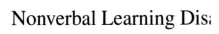

Nonverbal Learning Dis

John M. Davis · Jessica Broitman

Nonverbal Learning Disabilities in Children

Bridging the Gap Between Science and Practice

 Springer

John M. Davis
California State University, East Bay
25800 Carlos Bee Boulevard
Hayward, CA 94542-3095, USA
jack.davis@csueastbay.edu

Jessica Broitman
San Francisco Psychotherapy Research Group
Clinic and Training Center
9 Funston Street
San Francisco, CA 94129, USA
drjess@comcast.net

ISBN 978-1-4419-8212-4   e-ISBN 978-1-4419-8213-1
DOI 10.1007/978-1-4419-8213-1
Springer New York Dordrecht Heidelberg London

Library of Congress Control Number: 2011924678

Printed on acid-free paper

Springer is part of Springer Science+Business Media (www.springer.com)

To Jacob with love!

Foreword

The field of child psychology is continually evolving. Nonverbal learning disability (NVLD) is not currently recognized by the Diagnostic and Statistical Manual, yet research about NVLD is burgeoning. The number of publications concerning NVLD has risen from 15 in the years between 1981 and 1990 to 85 in the years 2001–2010 (Semrud-Clikeman, Fine, & Bledsoe, 2008). The clinical interest in NVLD has also increased with 14 articles submitted for publication concerning diagnosis NVLD in just the last 7 years. As interest has increased, our knowledge of the underlying etiology and diagnostic features of NVLD has expanded.

Unfortunately, efficacious treatments for children with NVLD have not progressed at the same rate, and most interventions that are published are based on anecdotal or clinical experience. It is important to collect such information in one volume so we can more fully evaluate the efficacy of such treatments and to begin to establish empirical bases for such treatment. This volume examines diagnostic criteria for NVLD and current knowledge about assessment and treatments for NVLD. As such, this book allows the practitioner to become aware of possible treatments and allows researchers to begin empirically validating these treatments. In addition, this book suggests new ways to conceptualize NVLD as a disorder with subtypes.

There are many thorny issues that are unresolved regarding the diagnosis of NVLD. As suggested in this volume, one important unresolved issue is knowledge of the differences between NVLD, high functioning autism, and Asperger's syndrome. Our current work at Michigan State University has identified differences between NVLD and Asperger's syndrome mainly in the areas of behavior but also in the academic area of math. In a recently completed large study conducted at our center, we found that children with NVLD significantly differed on measures of mathematical calculation as well as on visual-spatial organization when compared to children with Asperger's syndrome. While children with Asperger's syndrome did have difficulty with visual-spatial skills, the difficulty was not of the same magnitude as it was for children with NVLD. In addition, a comprehensive diagnostic interview (Autism Diagnostic Interview-Revised) with the main caretakers of these children revealed that children with NVLD scored within the normal range on all of the scales except social communication. In contrast, those with Asperger's syndrome had significant difficulty with stereotyped behaviors as well as with social reciprocity (Semrud-Clikeman, Fine, Bledsoe, Vroman, & Crow, 2010). The differentiation of

Asperger's syndrome (and likely high functioning autism) appears to rest on the presence of stereotyped or ritualistic behaviors.

We found that another characteristic difference between children with NVLD and children with Asperger's syndrome is the tendency of children with NVLD to be diagnosed solely on the basis of a verbal–performance-IQ-split or a mathematics delay (Semrud-Clikeman, Walkowiak, Wilkinson, & Christopher, 2010) yet a sizable minority of children with Asperger's also share these characteristics. Thus, it appears that making a diagnosis of NVLD based solely on these two characteristics (visual-spatial and VIQ>PIQ split) may result in a false diagnosis and children with Asperger's syndrome being misdiagnosed with NVLD (Semrud-Clikeman et al., 2010). Consequently, careful diagnosis, as described in this volume, is crucial for the appropriate classification and treatment of children with NVLD or with Asperger's syndrome.

Our recent large study of children with NVLD, Asperger's syndrome, and neurotypical children used functional magnetic resonance imaging (fMRI), and preliminary findings indicate that children with NVLD and Asperger's syndrome may appear neuropsychologically similar with comparable deficits in social perception, visual-spatial reasoning, and cognitive flexibility. However, our fMRI findings indicate that children with NVLD activate many more areas of their brain while solving a social problem compared to neurotypical children or children with Asperger's syndrome and these areas tend to be in the posterior region of the brain. In contrast children with Asperger's syndrome and those with no diagnosis show less activation in these regions with the typically developing children showing more right hemispheric activation than either the children with NVLD or with Asperger's syndrome. Such findings suggest that there may be differential brain networks that solve problems for each type of diagnosis. Further study is warranted to more fully understand the brain–behavior connections in NVLD as well as in Asperger's syndrome.

I believe that many school personnel as well as parents will find this volume helpful in working with their children to help ensure the child's eventual adjustment to adulthood. We surely need more research in this area particularly in the area of treatment and intervention. Some preliminary work has been completed that found creative drama to be efficacious for children with NVLD (Corbett & Glidden, 2000; Guli, Wilkinson, & Semrud-Clikeman, 2008) but more work is necessary. This book, which is the result of many years of clinical experience, provides an excellent overview of the current state of knowledge about NVLD for parents, educators, and professionals caring for children with this disorder.

Recent estimates have indicated that between 7 and 10% of the population have difficulties with social interaction and may be considered socially incompetent (Semrud-Clikeman, 2007). In an epidemiological study, approximately one-fifth of the population was found to show loneliness, anxiety, and shyness (Luanaigh & Lawlor, 2008). Although there has been a great deal of attention in recent years paid to verbal learning disabilities as well as to Attention Deficit Hyperactivity Disorder, problems with social functioning have not been as readily accepted particularly for special services in K-12 or in college. Moreover, poor social adaptation has been associated with subsequent cardiovascular difficulties as well as to psychiatric problems (Hawkley & Cacioppo, 2003).

There is also a great deal of current interest in the field of autism, and while reading and attention are important aspects of functioning, so is social adaptation. However, children with NVLD are often missed, not diagnosed, or not served and yet these children have similar needs to those who have a diagnosis of autism. I am hopeful that as the research and clinical writing concerning NVLD continues to expand, children and adults with this diagnosis will finally be provided the needed services and NVLD will be recognized as a legitimate disorder.

One clinical example of the effect of understanding the brain–behavior relationships in NVLD occurred spontaneously during an evaluation of a young man. He had just completed the fMRI task and I was walking him through the activation and structures that were on his MRI scan. I mentioned that he showed less activation in the right hemisphere – the hemisphere believed to be responsible for social understanding – compared to his brother who we had just also had an fMRI. His brother was developing typically. The young man remarked to me, "So my brain is abnormal," and I replied, "No it is just organized different. There is nothing abnormal on your scan." Two days later his mother contacted me and said, "Thank you so much for talking to my son. He came home and told his father I know now that I am not abnormal – my brain is just organized differently – Dr. Peg said so and I have pictures to prove it!" These types of interventions likely occur frequently but are undocumented. My experience as a pediatric neuropsychologist suggests that providing a therapeutic assessment involves not just explaining the results of the testing but also helping the client understand how the results may impact his/her life and which interventions might improve their adjustment. One of the goals of this current volume is to provide a blueprint for understanding NVLD as well as possible interventions that can be useful.

Books such as this one are needed to understand these disorders from a clinical standpoint as well as to put together the extant research. It is hoped that the diagnosis of NVLD will at some point be recognized by the Diagnostic and Statistical Manual as well as by the school systems as a disorder that can be very handicapping to the child and adolescent. As is so eloquently expressed in the afterword in this volume, understanding of this disorder by the person affected can be very therapeutic not only in the person's development but also in his/her eventual adult adaptation.

Michigan, USA   Margaret Semrud-Clikeman

References

Corbett, B. A., & Glidden, H. (2000). Processing affective stimuli in children with attention-deficit hyperactivity disorder. *Child Neuropsychology, 6*, 144–155.

Guli, L. A., Wilkinson, A., & Semrud-Clikeman, M. (2008). *Social competence intervention program*. Champaign, IL: Research Press.

Hawkley, L. C., & Cacioppo, J. T. (2003) Loneliness and pathways to disease. *Brain, Behavior, and Immunity, 17*(Supplement 1), S98–S105.

Luanaigh, C. O., & Lawlor, B. A. (2008). Loneliness and the health of older people. *International Journal of Geriatric Psychiatry, 23*, 1213–1221.

Semrud-Clikeman, M. (2007). *Social competence in children*. New York: Springer.

Semrud-Clikeman, M., Fine, J. G., & Bledsoe, J. (2008). *Meta-analysis of empirical literature on NVLD*. Paper presented at the International Neuropsychological Society.

Semrud-Clikeman, M., Fine, J. G., Bledsoe, J., Vroman, L., & Crow, S. (2010). *Asperger's disorder versus nonverbal learning disabilities: A diagnostic conundrum*. Paper presented at the National Academy of Neuropsychology.

Semrud-Clikeman, M., Walkowiak, J., Wilkinson, A., & Christopher, G. (2010). Neuropsychological findings in nonverbal learning disabilities. *Developmental Neuropsychology, 35*(5), 582–600.

Acknowledgments

We would like to thank Dr. Gibor Basri and Dr. Jodene Fine for their careful reading, editing, and overall support during the process of writing our book. Their thoughtful insights proved invaluable.

Contents

Chapter 1
Introduction and Overview

The purpose of this book is to help professionals to better understand and identify a subtype of a specific learning disability referred to in the literature as a nonverbal learning disorder and/or a nonverbal learning disability (NVLD). Such professionals might include school-based practitioners such as school psychologists, school counselors, school nurses, resource teachers, speech and language therapists, and occupational therapists, as well as the additional professionals who interact with them such as child psychiatrists, developmental pediatricians, clinical psychologists, social workers, and private therapists.

In Chapter 2 we provide a history of the evolution of this concept of NVLD. We also present the most widely used definition or diagnostic criteria (Rourke, 1985, 1989, 1995), as well as a clinical description and developmental orientation to this disorder.

In Chapter 3 we review the newer emerging theories which are beginning to consider NVLD as a disorder which has its own subtypes rather than being a unitary construct, as well as presenting our own four subtype model.

In Chapter 4 we address three primary issues. First, we explore three ideas about causes of learning disorders and of NVLD in particular. We review the available genetic, neurobiological, and environmental studies and theories. More specifically, in the genetics section we pay attention to the cytogenetic studies, genome searches, and candidate gene searches. In the neurobiology section we review studies associated with brain size, brain structure, and brain chemistry. In the environmental section we review issues such as obstetric suboptimality, pre-natal factors, and postnatal factors. Finally, we present the most current model of understanding NVLD from a neurological perspective, the "white matter model."

In Chapter 5 we discuss what is known regarding the prevalence of NVLD. Prevalence is discussed in relationship to gender, socioeconomic status, and other variables. In addition, we also explore the relationship to and co-occurrence of NVLD with other developmental disorders, such as AD/HD, and with psychiatric disorders, such as depression.

In Chapter 6 we explore the similarities and differences between Asperger's Disorder and NVLD as there remains considerable controversy regarding this issue.

J.M. Davis and J. Broitman, *Nonverbal Learning Disabilities in Children:*
Bridging the Gap Between Science and Practice, DOI 10.1007/978-1-4419-8213-1_1,
© Springer Science+Business Media, LLC 2011

In Chapter 7 we cover eligibility for special services. This includes brief overviews of both the Individuals with Disabilities Education Act – 2004 and Section 504 of the Rehabilitation Act of 1973.

In Chapter 8 we address screening for NVLD, including the Response to Intervention model. In addition, we present our model for the comprehensive psychoeducational assessment of NVLD.

In Chapter 9 we review and discuss the general guiding principles regarding treating children with NVLD. Evidence suggests that the earlier and more accurate the diagnosis coupled with early intervention, the better the outcome (Martin, 2007; Thompson, 1997). This chapter offers the general guiding principles regarding treating children with NVLD which best exemplify our philosophy and replicate our clinical experience.

In Chapter 10 we apply the general principles previously discussed to two settings: schools and the home. We present the views and suggestions of several clinicians who represent the best practices consistent with our model. In addition, we discuss the need for parent education and consultation with the goal of creating an inclusive "treatment team." The role of the school professional in providing or guiding these services is emphasized, and it is expected that this chapter will serve as a resource for all psychologists in developing recommendations for identified students.

Chapter 11 addresses the significant increase in interest in documenting effective interventions for the treatment of NVLD. This covers interventions for the most common difficulties associated with NVLD like mathematics, writing, and aspects of reading. In addition, we review what is known regarding speech and language, gross and fine motor, and social skills interventions. Given the impetus of the enactment of No Child Left Behind, it seems likely that this will become more important as practitioners will need to document that their interventions meet these standards and are being provided at the level of intensity required for success.

Finally, in Chapter 12 we offer our concluding remarks and summarize our suggestions for working with children with NVLD and their families.

We anticipate that this book will enable care providers to better collect, understand, and disseminate information about children who must cope with NVLD. By the end of the book professionals will see the advantage of participating on a team with a number of players with different skills and orientations. We trust that you will recognize that NVLD is a set of *life* issues, not just a school-based learning issue.

Chapter 2
History of the Concept of NVLD

The National Center for Education Statistics estimates that 20–25% of children will have learning disabilities (1998). "Specific learning disability" (SLD) is the most prevalent eligibility category in special education. SLD is a disorder in one or more of the central nervous system processes involved in perceiving, understanding, and/or using concepts through verbal (spoken or written) language or nonverbal means. The term does not include learning problems that are primarily the result of visual, hearing, or motor disabilities, of mental retardation, of emotional disturbance, or of environmental, cultural, or economic disadvantage (Federal guidelines 34 CFR 300.7).

SLD manifests itself with a deficit in one or more of the following areas: attention, reasoning, processing, memory, communication, reading, writing, spelling, calculation, coordination, social competence, and emotional maturity. Clinically children with SLD might have problems with *input*, or how they take in information through perception: auditory, visual, and tactile. Additionally the students might have difficulties with *integration*, or how they use new information, to understand novel concepts and to link new with extant ideas. They might find it difficult to understand an idea, start with small details and work up throughout every step, and combine multiple ideas. Lastly one might see problems with *output*, which is where a child shows what he or she has learned. Successful output includes not only oral and written expression, but also the ability to prepare information for output by ordering and organizing thoughts for cohesive communication of ideas.

Disorders often mentioned in this category include:

- *Dyslexia*. A language-based disability in which a person has trouble understanding written words. It may also be referred to as reading disability or reading disorder.
- *Dyscalculia*. A mathematical disability in which a person has a difficult time solving arithmetic problems and grasping math concepts.
- *Dysgraphia*. A writing disability in which a person finds it hard to form letters or write within a defined space.
- *Auditory and visual processing disorders*. Sensory disabilities in which a person has difficulty understanding language despite normal hearing and vision.
- *Nonverbal learning disabilities*. Problems with visual-spatial, intuitive, organizational, evaluative and holistic processing functions, and social/emotional issues.

J.M. Davis and J. Broitman, *Nonverbal Learning Disabilities in Children:*
Bridging the Gap Between Science and Practice, DOI 10.1007/978-1-4419-8213-1_2,
© Springer Science+Business Media, LLC 2011

Given this complexity, it is incumbent upon school psychologists and other support personnel, for example, resource teachers, speech and language therapists, school counselors, and occupational therapists (OTs), to know about *all of the subtypes* of learning disabilities. This is necessary so that we can identify, diagnose, understand, and intervene in the lives of these students to increase their chances of success in their school age and adult lives. While we currently know the most about dyslexia and ADHD, our understanding of nonverbal learning disability (NVLD) is considerably less well developed. Estimates vary about how prevalent NVLD is, but the most cited estimate is that 10–15% of all learning disabled students have a nonverbal learning disorder (Ozols & Rourke, 1988). It is imperative that practitioners know how to identify students who are at risk for, and manifest, this disorder. Although data have been accumulating since as far back as Johnson and Myklebust's (1967) classic work, *Learning Disabilities: Educational Principles and Practices*, nonverbal learning disabilities are still the least known and the least understood subtype. Although there has been increased interest in this disorder in the 1980s and 1990s, researchers and practitioners have not even been able to agree whether nonverbal learning disabilities should be abbreviated as NLD (mostly used on the West Coast) or NVLD (preferred by East Coast clinicians), nor have they arrived at an accepted definition, although Rourke's definition is the most noted (Pelletier, Ahmad, & Rourke, 2001). We have chosen to use the abbreviation NVLD for the purposes of this book.

Without knowledge or understanding, we run the risk of intervening in ways that are not helpful, or possibly even harmful to our students. As the reader will see over the course of this book there are many more associated features and symptoms of NVLD which need to be accounted for than in its language-based counterpart, dyslexia. Treatment is made even more complicated by the variety and number of different professionals who come into contact with children with NVLD.

For instance, the authors initiated a study in an urban hospital setting where we were trying to look at the effects of a particular intervention on spatial processing for students who met our study criteria for NVLD. This intervention was conducted in the child development unit and was primarily provided by occupational therapists. These occupational therapists more often than not referred to potential students with NVLD as children with "sensory integration" problems (Humphries, Krekewich, & Snider, 1996). The hospital also had a speech and language clinic that provided language and social skills interventions for children it tended to diagnose as experiencing "semantic/pragmatic" disorders (Volden, 2004). Likewise, there was a psychiatry department where students were being treated in groups for social skills deficits. The departments did not communicate across disciplines about these students, all of whom might have met our criteria for NVLD. This greatly inhibited our ability to find subjects, resulting in the termination of the research project. Our belief is that these same issues are also common to most schools and/ or school districts, resulting in poor continuity of care for students with NVLD. This is similar, as the reader will see, to the old adage about the blind men all touching different parts of the same elephant and calling them by different names, resulting in inconsistent and incomplete treatment.

To help readers develop a "feeling" for this disorder, let us review a clinician's concept of the child with NVLD. Judy Lewis' overview on the website NLDline. com, which is based on educator Sue Thompson's (1997) groundbreaking work, *The Source for Nonverbal Learning Disorders*, is a useful reference. Lewis lists early speech and vocabulary development, remarkable rote memory, strong auditory retention, attention to detail, at times good early reading skills, and excellent spelling skills as among the assets of some children with NVLD. Five major categories of deficits and dysfunction are identified: motor, visual-spatial, organizational, social, and sensory. Motor deficits include poor coordination, severe balance problems, and difficulties with graphomotor skills. Visual-spatial/ organizational deficits reflect a lack of image formation, poor visual recall, faulty spatial perceptions, and difficulties with executive functions. These executive functioning difficulties include decision making, planning, initiative, assigning priority, sequencing, motor control, emotional regulation, problem solving, planning, impulse control, establishing goals, monitoring results of action, self-correcting, and problems with spatial relations. Social deficits include difficulties comprehending nonverbal communication, adjusting to transitions and novel situations, along with deficits in social judgment and social interaction. The last category refers to sensitivity in any of the sensory modes: visual, auditory, tactile, taste, or olfactory.

Defining NVLD

As implied above, how NVLD is defined is crucial to how we assess, understand, and intervene for it. In contrast to dyslexia, NVLD is not currently in any formal eligibility or diagnostic codes such as the Diagnostic and Statistical Manual of Mental Disorders – IV-TR (2000) Or ICD-9 (2008). Some researchers do not view NVLD as a specific learning syndrome and argue against it even being considered as an "official" diagnosis (Pennington, 2009), while others argue that creating a formal diagnostic code will aid in the research and treatment of NVLD and for insurance reimbursement for services. At this point it does not seem likely that NVLD will be considered for DSM-V, which is in the planning stages for 2012 (Semrud-Clikeman, personal communication, 2009).

We assert that NLVD should be formalized, not only to aid research, but also to make it easier for parents to be able to receive benefits for intervention for the disorder. In addition, we believe that having a formalized diagnostic category will be a useful heuristic tool for guiding assessment and intervention. But let us begin with an historical perspective for how our understanding of the syndrome of NVLD has progressed over time.

Josef Gerstmann, an Austrian born neurologist, who fled Nazi Europe to the United States in the late 1930s, wrote the first published article on a syndrome consisting of symptoms very similar to what we now call nonverbal learning disorders. This syndrome, that eventually took his name, became the Gerstmann Syndrome (1940). He noted that this syndrome consisted of difficulties in the areas of finger agnosia (difficulty with information getting from and to the fingers), right–left orientation (confusion between right and left), agraphia (handwriting difficulties), and acalculia (math difficulties). He linked these nonverbal issues to problems in math and writing, but his primary focus was on sensorimotor and fine motor issues. Although NVLD is now more recently thought of as a right-hemisphere issue (Gross-Tsur, Shalev, Manor, & Amir, 1995; Semrud-Clikeman & Hynd, 1990), Gerstmann wrote that "the localizing value of the syndrome is significantly emphasized by the fact that the syndrome of finger angosia is represented in the brain unilaterally, and that (as in aphasia and apraxia) it is associated with a correspondingly located lesion in the dominant side of the brain, that is, the left-hemisphere in right-handed persons" (p. 405).

Johnson & Myklebust (1967) significantly furthered our thinking about NVLD in their book, *Learning Disabilities: Educational Principles and Practices.* In this work they described their version of the syndrome of nonverbal learning disorders. Whereas Gerstmann (1940) had noted fine motor difficulties and difficulties with math and writing, Johnson and Myklebust (1967) observed additional difficulties in visual-spatial processing and something they called "social perception." They suggested that children with these issues had difficulties in the following areas: understanding gesture, nonverbal motor learning, body image, spatial orientation, right–left orientation, and social perception. Additionally, these children also demonstrated distractibility, perseveration, and disinhibition. Later work has also found overlap with ADHD and executive function issues (Landau, Gross-Tsur, Auerback, Van der Meere, & Shalev, 1999). Johnson and Mykelbust's vision generally holds true to current thinking about NVLD.

The next major advances in research and thinking about NVLD were made by Byron Rourke and his many colleagues. He is the leading exponent of the dominant model and/or definition of NVLD today. After decades of research and two seminal books, *Neuropsychology of Learning Disabilities: Essentials of Subtype Analysis* (1985) and *Syndrome of Nonverbal Learning Disabilities: Neurodevelopmental Manifestations* (1995), Rourke has left a significant mark on the field both by trying to establish a diagnostic set of criteria for NVLD and offering a theory for the cause of the disorder.

Rourke's diagnostic criteria have remained fairly stable over time. Most recently, Rourke and his colleagues (Pelletier et al., 2001) have stated that the following criteria have to be met to determine NVLD:

1. Target test at least 1 SD below the mean.
2. No, or very minimal, simple tactile imperception and suppression versus very poor finger agnosia and/or finger dysgraphesthesia.
3. The highest scores on two subtests of the Verbal Scale of the Wechsler Intelligence Scale for Children-III (WISC-III): Vocabulary, Similarities, or Information.
4. Two of the subtests from the WISC-III nonverbal subtests of Block Design, Object Assembly, or Coding fall among the lowest scores of the Performance scale.

5. Wide Range Achievement Test–Revised (WRAT–R) standard score for Reading is at least 8 points higher than Arithmetic.
6. Tactual Performance Test, right, left, and both hand times become progressively worse vis-à-vis the norms.
7. Normal to superior grip strength versus mildly to moderately impaired Grooved Pegboard.
8. WISC-III: VIQ exceeds PIQ by at least 10 points.

The following conditions meet Rourke's criteria for a "diagnosis" of NVLD:

- Children presenting with the first six criteria would definitely be diagnosed with NVLD.
- Seven or eight of the features present would constitute a positive diagnosis.
- Five or six criteria suggest probable NVLD.
- Three or four criteria suggest questionable NVLD.
- One or two criteria suggest low probability of NVLD.

Those of us who do assessments will find problems with Rourke's algorithm. First, all of the instruments would be considered outdated today. Second, although many newer, better standardized tests are available, none have been utilized to update the definition. These are things that the authors will take up in later chapters.

A Developmental Orientation

In this section we offer a look at how a child with NVLD might manifest at different developmental stages. We briefly address signs of NVLD in early (preschool) development, early schooling, later elementary and middle school, and high school. It is important to note that the presenting symptoms change across development and are often difficult to identify.

Early Developmental Signs of NVLD

Piaget (Inhelder & Piaget, 1964) refers to his first stage of development as the sensorimotor stage, whereby much of learning is about the child's interactions with his/her environment and a sensory level. However, this is less likely for an NVLD child. As Rourke (1995) notes, others noted that the first developmental stage is sensorimotor. In describing NVLD children, "these children remain essentially sedentary, exploring the world not through vision or locomotion, but rather through receiving verbal answers to questions posed about the immediate environment" (p. 8). The disparity between precocious language development, especially vocabulary, and the delays in motor development in the child is most notable in the early years.

Anecdotal reports from parents of children with NVLD often state that their children would sit and point at an object, saying what they wanted rather than crawling toward it. In anticipation of normal exploration, one parent spoke of how she "baby-proofed" her house to protect her child, yet her child never crawled to or tried to open anything. Many of these children do not use typical toddler toys or enjoy coloring or drawing. They are usually disinterested in or unable to put puzzles together (Johnson, 1987a). Parents are often confused when their extremely verbal child is not developing consistently across developmental lines. They may create unwarranted and inaccurate expectations, based upon inappropriate assumptions about their child's superior language development. Problems for the child can become exacerbated when poor motor and spatial development can disappoint and confound the parents.

Early sensorimotor exploration is important in the child's development, since learning depends upon the interaction of the child with the environment (Piaget, 1972). The brain develops secondary to its interactions with the environment developing neural networks that then create efficiency. Although NVLD children are interacting with their environment, it is often more verbal and observational and less motoric and spatial, which alters development of the neural networking. As the old saying goes, "neurons that fire together wire together." It is likely that less interaction and practice exploring the environment with the body may lead to less efficiency in motor skills compared to children with many more hours of practice. In turn, as they grow older, children with less confidence in their motor skills may be less inclined to engage in activities demanding it, further reducing their skill growth and development.

When clumsiness is deemed significant by a parent or a preschool teacher, consultation with a pediatrician or physical therapist may be recommended.

Early Schooling

Kindergarten teachers may notice problems in fine motor skills that have not been noted earlier in a child with NVLD. The child may struggle more than his or her peers with items such as scissors, crayons, or pencils. As demands for writing and drawing increase, the teacher may notice immaturity in the child with NVLD compared to typically developing peers.

The teacher may turn to an occupational therapist (OT) for consultation and guidance. After observing the child, the OT might provide an evaluation or offer treatment. Sensory Integration Therapy (Ayres, 1994) might be offered to treat what the OT views as a sensory integration disorder. If the child's issues are in the mild to moderate range, this may be all that is offered.

Sometimes children with NVLD may be referred for help with non-phonological reading difficulties (Pennington, 1991), but intervention may be premature.

Rourke (1995) notes that these difficulties may well be developmental for children with NVLD, and most children with NVLD develop basic reading skills without intervention. However, David Gresham (Griffin & Gresham, 2002) theorizes that these reading problems are often associated with difficulties in visual processing problems, like tracking. Tracking refers to the ability of the child to stay on the correct line of reading or math without veering off course creating confusion and extra time for the student to reorient oneself. Gresham suggests that these problems are due to visual-spatial processing difficulties. He claims that NVLD children frequently require tracking training, and that 30% of NVLD children need to be retrained to read fluently. He suggests performing a thorough optometric examination that includes an assessment of visual tracking.

Often, children with NVLD develop early math difficulties, although some use their verbal memory strengths to help them compensate through third grade, and occasionally beyond. If not earlier, during this period concerns begin to develop about social perception and pragmatic language development. Further, boys and girls with NVLD can present with clinical signs of anxiety, depression, attention problems, obsessional preoccupations, and self-esteem problems (Palombo & Berenberg, 1999). It remains unclear whether children with NVLD experience difficulties with peers because of processing issues, for example, difficulty processing facial expressions and social signals, executive function difficulties, novel problem solving, or due to another reason. They might even result from reduced interaction with peers due to their sensorimotor issues (Hale & Fiorello, 2004). Clearly further research is required to evaluate these hypotheses.

With difficulties in the social area, especially with pragmatic language problems, the next professional to become involved is most often a speech and language therapist. During earlier stages these children might have been seen for articulation issues connected with poor oromotor functions, while in early elementary school they are more likely seen for pragmatic language difficulties in social discourse. Children with NVLD often do not use appropriate vocal intonations. They might speak in a flat monotone or with a sing-song voice. It can be difficult to read their mood from their facial expressions and they may seem wooden and constricted (Palombo & Berenberg, 1999). In speech and language nomenclature these issues are often called "semantic–pragmatic" disorders (Volden, 2004). It is believed to bode well for youngsters if these issues are identified early and intervention begins before the child falls behind allowing secondary features, especially anxiety, to develop (Palombo & Berenberg, 1999).

Even though children may struggle and become frustrated by math and written expression, they tend not to be referred to special educators because they perform "well enough." Their superior verbal skills often cause educators and parents to assume that their difficulties arise from insufficient effort, or difficulty paying attention. Rourke (1995) wrote that young children with these symptoms are often misdiagnosed with ADHD. Unfortunately such misdiagnoses can lead to a host of self-esteem problems and psychological issues, particularly when appropriate interventions are withheld.

Later Elementary and Middle School Signs

As academic subjects become more abstract, and more independent work is expected, NVLD children often begin to experience greater difficulties. Executive function problems increase. At the same time more demands are placed on social skills creating significant additional stress and frustration that can elevate anxiety and which also makes academic progress difficult.

At this point academically oriented professionals often become involved in the lives of NVLD children. Teachers become alarmed and mention their concerns at parent conferences. Parents ask for help for their children and wheels are set in motion. In either case, some variation of a Student Study Team (SST) is requested. School staff and sometimes parents gather to problem solve new ways of working with the child. These discussions can result in recommendations and/or interventions within the classroom. In public schools these concerns can also lead to a psychoeducational evaluation of the child. If testing reveals that the child is eligible for other special services, either under IDEA-04 or Section 504 of the Rehabilitation Act of 1973, an Individualized Education Plan (IEP) or Section 504 Plan could be developed to detail more specific ways of working with the child based on the available data (see Chapter 7 for more details) (Hale & Fiorello, 2004; Telzrow & Bonar, 2002).

Providing the best assistance for the student can become problematic because so much depends upon who gets involved and what they already know. The child's parents also need to educate themselves to become more knowledgeable as they will become increasingly involved in their child's treatment team. Helpful books for parents include: Sue Thompson's *The Source for Nonverbal Learning Disorders* (1997), Pamela Tanguay's *Nonverbal Learning Disorders at Home* (2001) or *Nonverbal Learning Disorders at School* (2002), Kathy Allen's *Star Shaped Pegs, Square Holes: Nonverbal Learning Disorders and the Growing Up Years* (1998), and Rondalyn Whitney's *The Nonverbal Learning Disorder Guide for Teachers, Parents, Employers, and Therapists* (2000). The SST or IEP team could advise them to join the Nonverbal Learning Disorders Association (http://www.nlda.org) or to become familiar with websites such as Judy Lewis's http://www.nldline.com, Pam Tanguay's http://www.NLDontheweb.org, or Charles Schwab's website, http://www.schwablearning.org. More information related to working with the families will be provided in a later chapter.

High School Signs

If the child with NVLD has managed to navigate the comprehensive middle school environment, the high school experience becomes the next challenge. During high school, social skills can become a source of even greater concern, as social stresses, such as the demands of dating, are increased. Advanced math and sciences will also be more challenging. Increased demands on executive functioning, as in written expression and advanced reading skills, can present severe challenges. Research is mixed regarding whether students with NVLD are more at risk for psychiatric disorders, like depression with some finding increased levels of depression (Brumbach, 1985; Fletcher, 1989; Rourke, Young, & Leenaars, 1989) and other not finding that children with NVLD are at increased risk for psychiatric disorders (Mokros, Poznanski, & Merrick, 1989). It is possible that these contradictory findings are be due to the significant differences in age groups, race, and income among the different studies (or differing definitions for diagnosis given the wide range of diagnostic criteria used in research on NVLD). However, with interventions, accommodations, and modifications students with NVLD are often able to tap into their skill sets and experience success as emphasized by Brooks (1991) and his concept of "islands of competence." By this he is referring to the fact that learning-disabled students have relative strengths and weaknesses and that it is at least equally important that the student's strengths get recognized and enhanced as it is to remediate any relative weaknesses or deficits. Skill sets might include acquisition of a second language, drama, certain aspects of the arts, language arts, and some of the language-based sciences.

Generally the support team continues to be involved in the student's program, if not via the IEP process then sometimes utilizing the Section 504 laws. Transition planning becomes essential and decisions about further education need to be made. In our experience, students who have not become too demotivated, depressed, or demoralized can move on to successful adulthood if they, with the help of their parents and coaches, choose wisely with special regard for their strengths. Students with NVLD often interact better with adults than with their peers. Personal accounts written by people with NVLD suggest that adulthood may bring more successful interactions and relationships. Debbie Green, for example, in *Growing up with NLD* (1999) writes of her joys as a teacher. Laurie E. Reed talks of her career as an occupational therapist in *Unaware: Living with Non-verbal Learning Disabilities* (2001). These authors emphasize that early accurate diagnosis and appropriate intervention are crucial to the well-being of the person with NVLD.

Summary

In this chapter we have offered an overview of the history of the development and understanding of nonverbal learning disorders. The most commonly used definition has been reviewed and we have considered how the child with NVLD might appear at different developmental stages. Next in Chapter 3 we will discuss advances in our current thinking about NVLD and the possibility that NVLD is not one disorder but rather has subtypes.

Chapter 3
NVLD and Subtypes

Historically, Rourke (1985, 1991) and others (Drummond, Ahmad, & Rourke, 2005; Harnadek & Rourke, 1994; Johnson & Myklebust, 1967; Pennington, 1991) spent a significant amount of time clarifying the differences between what are often referred to as verbal or phonologically based learning disorders and nonverbal learning disorders. More recently, some theorists have suggested that, as with many developmental disorders, NVLD should be considered as a disorder with different subtypes (Davis & Broitman, 2007; Forrest, 2004; Grodzinsky, 2003; Mamen, 2006). This notion fits with our clinical experience. This chapter reviews the most recent developments in the understanding of NVLD as a disorder with multiple subtypes or components.

Researchers such as Semrud-Clikeman (2001) and others (Forrest, 2004; Myklebust, 1975) continue to view NVLD somewhat differently than Rourke. Without citing specific numbers, Semrud-Clikeman suggests that only some of the strengths and weaknesses proposed by Rourke need to be present for a child to be diagnosed with NVLD. More recently, a study by Wilkinson and Semrud-Clikeman (2008) found no differences between children with NVLD and those without NVLD on measures of sensory and tactile measures. Further, Semrud-Clikeman and her group found that other measures such as social perception (Fine, Semrud-Clikeman, Reynolds, & Smith, in preparation) and measures of cognitive flexibility and fluid reasoning can also contribute to a differential diagnosis (Semrud-Clikeman & Glass, 2008). Thus, it appears that all symptoms listed by earlier studies do not carry the same weight for a diagnosis of NVLD. This supports our view that various permutations with these symptoms may result in different behavioral manifestation of the disorder, or subtypes, and that the diagnostic criteria are still evolving. Further study is needed to better understand whether these possible subtypes are phenotypically distinct or whether there is overlap among them; however, subtype models of NVLD are presently being considered. We will review four clinicians' current proposed subtypes followed by our own model.

Forrest (2004), Grodzinsky (2003), Mamen (2002), and Palombo (2006) suggest that there are specific clinical subtypes of NVLD that are important to understand in order to diagnose and treat the child or adult appropriately. A developmental analogy to this would be similar to the current definition of ADHD, which has

J.M. Davis and J. Broitman, *Nonverbal Learning Disabilities in Children:*
Bridging the Gap Between Science and Practice, DOI 10.1007/978-1-4419-8213-1_3,
© Springer Science+Business Media, LLC 2011

evolved to include the inattentive, hyperactive/impulsive, and combined types. Rourke however, disagrees, calling it a "confusion of the syndrome of NVLD (its neurodevelopmental assets, deficits and dynamics) with its most predominant behavioral (essentially, 'dependent variable') manifestations" (Rourke, http://www. NLD-BPROURKE.CA). According to Rourke these differences are variations in the expression of NVLD. Since we have no available data documenting that visual-spatial issues alone are responsible for these differences, multiple lines of development, along the lines proposed by Howard Gardner (1999), could prove to be another valuable model from which to conceptualize the various manifestations of NVLD. We therefore suggest that it is important to expose school personnel who are diagnosing, treating, and educating children with NVLD to viable alternatives of ways of understanding NVLD. We believe this would help ensure that the NVLD student is getting appropriate interventions for success in school and in life.

The clinical models presented here consist of a two-subtype model (Forrest, 2004), a three-subtype model (Grodzinsky, 2003), and two four-subtype models (Mamen, 2002; Palombo, 2006). Although some of the models overlap, we will describe the characteristics for each of the most relevant subtypes and offer an overall integration. We will describe some of the strengths of these children and review the neuropsychological, social, and academic concerns for each subtype. Although we will be incorporating Palombo's model, its emphasis on social and psychological issues rather than neuropsychological and academic issues renders it less applicable for our purposes here. It is however an excellent resource for mental health practitioners in the school system who are responsible for knowing more about the psychological and social issues related to NVLD children and their treatment. We will then talk about how we would bring these together in a model which we would espouse.

Two-Subtype Model of NVLD

The two-subtype model describes a child who has a visual-spatial or perceptual disorder in addition to a social-skill deficit with or without a math problem (Forrest, 2004; Grodzinsky, 2003; Mamen, 2002). These authors do not believe that the NVLD child must have significant math problems, as described by Rourke (1995), and Palombo does not incorporate any academic issues into his model. Forrest (2004) suggests that the social skills disorders are caused by the visual-spatial deficits.

Although Forrest is the primary proponent of this model, she expresses some concerns. She suggests that this conceptualization of NVLD can confuse the differential diagnosis with Asperger's Disorders but that distinguishing characteristics can aid in the differential diagnosis (Forrest, 2004). For example, she notes that while both the child with NVLD and the one with Asperger's are interested in having social relationships, the NVLD child tends to be more successful as his/her social relationship issues are milder. NVLD children do not have the very narrow, intense, obsessional interests associated with Asperger's. Klin, Sparrow, Cicchetti and

Rourke (1995), however, presented evidence that Asperger's Disorder is a developmental disorder that is comorbid with the neurological profile of NVLD. Their approach integrates the psychiatric or developmental perspective with the neuropsychological one. They suggest that the name of this disorder depends upon who is doing the naming.

Palombo (2006) would agree that visual-spatial problems, which he calls non-linguistic perceptual deficits, create social imperception problems just as Johnson and Myklebust said before him. He claims that these nonlinguistic perceptual deficits are the core deficits in all NVLD children. He does not however believe that NVLD children are on the Autistic spectrum. We will address the NVLD, Asperger's, and autism similarities and differences more thoroughly in Chapter 4. He is the only one of the four clinicians we review to hypothesize that there are subtypes of NVLD children who suffer from additional problems of social relatedness and reciprocity that are not related to visual-spatial issues. He calls these social cognition impairments which he would include in a separate subtype that also includes reciprocal social relations, verbal and nonverbal language, and affective processing problems.

The two-subtype model is useful in highlighting the math problems, although Forrest (2004) agrees with the work of Keller and Sutton (1991) who suggest that the Wide Range Achievement Test (WRAT) measures math calculation only, not broader math skills. Since on this test one cannot determine whether the students performed poorly on math due to time limits, lining up numbers, or calculation, it remains unclear what kinds of math problems NVLD students' face. In fact, utilizing Rourke's (2000) data for the most recent criteria of NVLD, only 72% of the children he diagnosed with NVLD exhibited poor math skills, at least as measured by the WRAT-R. Based on these results, one can conclude that math skill deficits are not present in all children with NVLD. Therefore the two-subtype model is conceptualized as a visual-spatial processing problem which creates social skill deficits with a possible comorbid math problem.

Neurological, Social and Academic Concerns for the Two-Subtype Model

The NVLD child with a visual-spatial or perceptual disorder might have problems in nonverbal reasoning, processing, output, and some aspects of language. The typical nonverbal reasoning difficulties are in the areas of visual constructional reasoning, pattern analysis and synthesis, and nonverbal problem solving, especially with new or novel information. Processing difficulties might include visual and tactile perception, visual and spatial memory, visual attention, and fine and gross motor development (Pennington, 1991; Rourke 1995). There is research that suggests that there are differences between spatial-simultaneous and spatial-sequential memory (Mammarella, Cornoldi, Pazzaglia, Toso, Grimoldi, et al., 2006). Output difficulties affect handwriting, executive functions, and production in general.

Children with NVLD tend to have strengths related to language, including verbal reasoning, rote verbal learning, simple verbal span memory, oral expression, and phonological processing. However, speech and language pathologists often find that these children have semantic/pragmatic disorders (Volden, 2004). Socially, these children are viewed as naïve, talkative, and have issues involving body or personal space. They may engage in parallel play longer than their peers. They fare better in social relationships, especially in one-to-one situations, than children with Asperger's or autistic syndromes. Academically, they tend to be good at decoding, they read fluently with detail-oriented comprehension, and they spell phonetically. Their academic weaknesses tend to be in spatially oriented sciences, geography, and geometry. However, a common confusion that can lead to misdiagnosis stems from many NVLD children's difficulty with early reading, out of which they may develop into competent readers (Pennington, 1991a; Rourke, 1995).

Three-Subtype Model of NVLD

Grodzinsky (2003), Mamen (2002), and Palombo (2006) suggest a three-subtype model. They agree with Forrest (2004) regarding the spatial subtype with social problems and define it similarly, and that these children often have math difficulties related to aspects of visual-spatial processing. However, each proposes a third subtype that significantly overlaps with each other. Although they have chosen different names for this third subtype, the characteristics they describe are almost the same and include the social, visual processing speed, and attentional domains. This third subtype emphasizes the overlap between attention and executive function issues presented by both ADHD, especially the inattentive subtype, and NVLD. More specifically this NVLD subtype emphasizes the output disorder aspects of executive function issues as related to academics and how these issues can also impact social skills.

Neurological, Social, and Academic Concerns for the Three-Subtype Model

In this subtype, Grodzinsky, Mamen, and Palombo all focus on social deficits in describing neuropsychological subtypes of NVLD. They note a difference between verbal and nonverbal test scores, though spatial perception seems to be intact. For instance, Mamen (2002) writes about how on the Wechsler Intelligence Scale for Children: 3rd edition (Wechsler, 1991) you could find that Object Assembly and Picture Arrangement are relative weaknesses while the Block Design task is spared due to what she describes as the more socially oriented themes of the Object Assembly and Picture Arrangement subtests, although this is not necessarily what we authors have observed. She reports that social problems are related to expressive body language, pragmatic communication, personal or social space, and difficulties with prosody, humor, metaphor, and analogy. Academically, relative strengths are seen in reading although some NVLD students struggle with advanced reading comprehension. Often math skills are in the average to low average ranges, due to problems with attention to detail and procedural memory. In terms of written language, these children can be good at narrative discourse, but experience difficulty in expository writing where they have trouble anticipating the reader's needs.

All three authors also refer to poor attention span and/or internal and external distractibility, here most often associated with visual processing rather than attention per se. Executive functioning challenges are also noted in perseveration or cognitive inflexibility, self-regulation, processing speed, and accuracy. One example presented by Mamen (2002) is that the major "nonverbal" deficit on the WISC-III is that the Processing Speed Index score can be lower than the perceptual reasoning index but, contrary to much of the data on ADHD, both are lower than the Freedom from Distractibility Index of the WISC-III. This differs from Rourke's model, which relies on finding a significant discrepancy between verbal and nonverbal reasoning scores. We find that the descriptions above are similar to descriptions of attention deficit/hyperactivity disorder: inattentive subtype. Grodzinsky's model (2003) states that these children are very often viewed as hypoactive. Another similarity is that children with the inattentive subtype are often described as having issues with executive functioning and slow or "sluggish" cognitive tempos (Teeter & Semrud-Clikeman, 1997), evidenced by their frequently slow Processing Speed Index scores.

Children with NVLD may also appear somewhat rigid, though they function reasonably well in familiar settings. They may have a good sense of humor tending toward puns and word play yet can be seen as silly and somewhat immature compared to their same age peers. Basic reading skill development might be slow due to visual processing inefficiency that impedes learning the orthographic features of letters and words. They can do poorly on rapid naming tests (Grodzinsky, 2003). Once they "catch on" or have *overlearned* the letters they become fluent readers. Writing is often difficult and these children are characterized as poor or variable spellers, disorganized in their written language, with trouble monitoring their output. In math they may have some difficulty retrieving facts but they generally have average conceptual ability.

Four-Subtype Model of NVLD

A fourth neurological subtype is postulated only by Mamen (2002). She calls it a written expressive: nonverbal learning disability subtype that manifests primarily as a nonverbal disorder that should be included within the NVLD framework.

As stated above, Palombo's fourth subtype deals with social reciprocity which he views as also related to autistic spectrum disorders rather than the specific neurological deficits which we explore here.

Neurological, Social, and Academic Concerns

The main neuropsychological difficulty noted in subtype four is visual–motor integration, especially in timed situations, as on the WISC-IV Coding subtest. Mamen suggests that the Coding subtest yields lower scores than the Symbol Search subtest in this subtype. She describes the primary academic difficulties as dysgraphia or difficulty writing fluently, or copying letters or words rapidly, making it an output disorder. Mamen also describes what she believes are the social aspects of this disorder. They include low self-esteem, low frustration tolerance, and behavior or anger management issues. Mamen sees these social–emotional issues as secondary rather than primary and believes they may stem from a temperamental predisposition plus frustration.

Our Subtype Model

From our review of the existing models, along with our clinical experience, we believe that a four-subtype model has the most clinical relevance. We also believe that NVLD can best be viewed as a "spectrum" disorder. Children can have mild versions of some problems, for example, present without a specific functional impairment. Our observations suggest that the lack of functional impairment is mediated by overall intellectual potential, level of discrepancies between verbal and nonverbal measures, and parenting/intervention strategies which have enhanced coping mechanisms. It is our contention that all children who present with NVLD have significant visual-spatial and executive function difficulties. Therefore we consider these deficits to be the primary components of NVLD, constituting our first and core subtype. Children in this subtype may also have mild social and academic deficits. Our second subtype includes children with visual-spatial and executive function difficulties that significantly impact their social functioning. These children need formal evaluations and treatment programs, e.g., pragmatic language therapy and social skills training. Our third subtype is characterized by children with significant visual-spatial and executive function difficulties and functionally impacted academic problems. Again, the academic problems are primarily math-related but they can also affect advanced reading comprehension, written expression (especially expository), geography, and the math-related sciences. Our fourth and final subtype is characterized by children with visual-spatial, executive function, social difficulties, and academic deficits where all areas are functionally impaired. We do not believe that these are the only possible subtypes of NVLD, and ongoing research should pursue other possible models (Fig. 3.1).

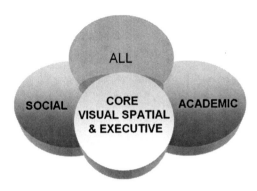

Fig. 3.1 Davis–Broitman model of NVLD

Summary

In our view any assessment or remedial plan for an NVLD child has to account for all the above-mentioned subtypes. However, we also believe that as more data accumulate, a multidimensional model may at some time seem a more appropriate metaphor for NVLD than a subtyping model. Therefore, the SST or IEP teams for children with suspected NVLD should consist of a school psychologist to look at the intellectual, neuropsychological/processing, and executive function issues, a special education teacher for the academic concerns, a speech and language pathologist for the semantic/pragmatic difficulties, and an occupational therapist for possible fine/gross motor difficulties. Other professionals might include a school counselor for social skills interventions and a referral to a child psychiatrist or developmental pediatrician for possible medication issues.

The most important concept we would like for the reader to take from this book is that nonverbal learning issues are more complex than we once thought. A differential diagnosis for NVLD must consider these subtypes, as well as other developmental and psychiatric disorders, dismissing areas where there is no evidence of dysfunction and formulating appropriate treatment plans where difficulties are found. In Chapter 4 we will review the available genetic, neurobiological, and environmental studies and theories regarding the etiology of NVLD.

Chapter 4
The Etiology of NVLD

In this chapter we will discuss the extent of our knowledge, as well as our uncertainty, regarding the causes of NVLD. Unfortunately, as is the case with other learning disabilities (LD: Duane, 1991) and developmental disorders (DD: Ozonoff & Rogers, 2003), the exact cause or causes of nonverbal learning disabilities are not yet clear. We review the current available information from the areas typically addressed when considering causality: genetics, neurobiology, and environment. Finally, the current model of understanding NVLD, which is commonly called the "white matter model" from a neurological perspective, will be presented.

Genetics

Studies focusing on the genetics of any disorder tend to fall into three areas: cytogenetic studies, genome searches, and candidate gene searches. Cytogenetic studies examine chromosomes for mutations outside of the normal structure, including deletions of genes, abnormal repetitions of genetic sequences, extra chromosomes, and entirely missing chromosomes. Some disorders can be inherited genetically, and others occur due to random mutation. Studies such as these have been done for a number of disorders like learning disabilities (Pennington, Bender, Puck, Salbenblatt, & Robinson, 1982), reading disabilities (DeFries, Fulker, & LaBuda, 1987; Raskin, 2001), and ADHD (Willcut, Pennington, & DeFries, 2000). Although none of these studies support a one chromosome extra disorder as, for example, Trisomy 21 does for Down's syndrome (Butler & Meaney, 2005), these studies are more realistically thought of in terms of establishing risk factors.

While there have been no such studies of NVLD as a developmental disorder, there are certain genetic disorders that do present with NVLD symptoms. Pennington (2009) makes a strong case for Turner's and Fragile X syndromes as presenting the classic symptoms of NVLD. Likewise, arguments have been made for other syndromes, such as 22q11.2 deletion syndrome (velocardiofacial/ DeGeorge syndrome) (Bearden, Woodin, Wang, Moss, McDonald-McGinn et al., 2001; Simon, 2008; Woodin, Wang, Aleman, McDonald-McGinn, Zackai et al., 2001), William's syndrome (Anderson & Rourke, 1995), de Lange syndrome (Tsatsanis

J.M. Davis and J. Broitman, *Nonverbal Learning Disabilities in Children: Bridging the Gap Between Science and Practice*, DOI 10.1007/978-1-4419-8213-1_4, © Springer Science+Business Media, LLC 2011

& Rourke, 1995), and Asperger's syndrome (Klin, Sparrow, Volkmar, Cicchetti, & Rourke, 2000b). In each of these syndromes there is some evidence for genetic predispositions; however, the presentation of NVLD symptoms is not so "classic" or consistent among these.

Although it is clear that these genetic disorders do present with NVLD symptoms, it is also true that clinicians have reported cases of NVLD without being associated with these kinds of known genetic disorders (e.g. Hale & Fiorello, 2004). Simon (2007) notes that "the visuospatial, visuomotor, and numerical impairments in WS, TS, FXS, and chromosome 22q11.2 deletion syndromes are striking in their degree of overlap and puzzling in that other commonalities are limited" (p. 603). One could argue that these findings currently are somewhat supportive of Rourke's (1989) "white matter model" discussed below, which suggests that NVLD is the result of white matter damage, the *cause* of which can come from multiple sources, most of which is in the right hemisphere and corpus callosum, rather than it being a *causative* disorder in and of itself. Or in other words, NVLD is the *phenotype* which may be the expression of a number of different *genotypes*. A genotype is the genetic constitution of an individual and the phenotype the observable properties of an organism produced by the interaction of the genotype and the environment.

Another genetic area of research is referred to as genome searches. These types of studies attempt to examine genetic material of families which include individuals with the disorder of interest. Two of the more prominent labs looking at theses issues for reading and language-based disorders are the Colorado Reading Project (DeFries, Olson, Pennington, & Smith, 1991) and the group at the University of Washington (Berningner & Richards, 2002). These sorts of studies have not yet been implemented for NVLD and thus currently we have no sense of the heritability factor for NVLD as a developmental disorder.

The last category of genetically oriented research is the candidate gene searches. These start with a prediction that certain genes are implicated based on clinical or empirical evidence which then looks for associations between and/or among the genes and the disorder. A fairly large body of data is beginning to be generated in areas such as mild mental retardation or intellectual challenge (Higgins, Pucilowski, Lombardi, & Rooney, 2004), dyslexia (Cope, Harold, Hill, Moskivina, Stevenson et al., 2005; Francks, Parachini, Smith, Richardson, Scerri, et al., 2004), and ADHD (Fisher, Francks, McCracken, McGough, Marlow, et al., 2002; Hawi, Segurado, Conroy, Sheehan, Lowe, et al., 2005), among others. Again, it seems likely that many different genes will be implicated for NVLD but these studies are yet to be materialized.

Neurobiology

The areas most often reviewed when considering the impact of neurobiology on a particular syndrome or developmental disorder are the size of the brain, the structures within the brain, and neurotransmitters. As above, we have no specific studies looking into these areas for NVLD as a developmental disorder, but we provide a brief review of other disorders to investigate whether there may be some overlapping areas of interest.

Probably the best replicated findings relating to brain size have to do with autism. Even in Kanner's (1943) early work he began talking about macrocephaly, reporting large head circumferences in about 25% of his child clients with autism. See also Sacco, Militerni, Frolli, Bravaccio, and Gritti et al. (2007) for a recent review of head circumference in autism. Two possible factors associated with this have been discussed. First, postmortem studies suggest a problem with cell migration leading to improper lamination of the layers of the brain. Second, there is evidence of precocious dendritic arborization, coupled with failure to prune (Amaral et al., 2008). In an excellent review and meta-analysis of structural MRI data on autism and brain structures, Stanfield and colleagues concluded that "autism is associated with generalized enlargements of the cerebral hemispheres, the cerebellum and the caudate nucleus; with reductions in the size of the corpus callosum and possibly the midbrain and vermal lobules" (Stanfield, McIntosh, Spencer, Philip, Gaur, & Lawrie, 2008). They also believe that these features/findings are related to the cardinal features of autism. However, here and throughout, we must be mindful that these differences are not necessarily *causative* but at least create a reasonable hypothesis.

ADHD has also been well studied in the area of brain structures. The cerebellum (Berquin, Giedd, Jacobsen, Hamburger, Krain, et al., 1998; Mostofsky, Reiss, Lockhart, & Denckla, 1998) has received attention. Often thought of as almost a "brain within a brain," it seems to be involved in coordinating cognitive functions which impact learning and memory, among other things (Ivry, 1993). However, other systems, such as the prefrontal cortex, the globus pallidus, the caudate (Pennington, 2009), and the putamen (Wellington, Semrud-Clikeman, Gregory, Murphy, & Lancaster, 2006), have all been implicated. As with autism, these areas create more hypotheses than conclusions at this time.

In the research on dyslexia, early concerns focused on the planum temporale, with the left planum temporale often being associated with phonological coding (Galaburda, Sherman, Rosen, Aboitiz, & Geschwind, 1985). Later research has been mixed, with some results supporting those initial findings (Larson, Hoien, Lundberg, & Odegaard, 1990; Morgan, 1997) and some not (Best & Demb, 1999; Robichon, Levrier, Farnarier, & Habib, 2000). Interestingly, as with ADHD, the cerebellum has also been implicated (Eckert, Leonard, Richards, Aylward, Thomson, & Berninger, 2003; Kronbichler, Wimmer, Staffen, Hutzler, Mair, et al., 2008).

The cerebellum may also be implicated in NVLD. If we use William's and Turner's syndromes as *models* for NVLD, Press, Murakami, Courchesne, Grafe, & Hesselink (1990) found that the average cerebral volumes were significantly smaller for William's syndrome adults vs. controls. Steinlin (2007) reported that in her patients with congenital nonprogressive ataxia, a congenital malformation of the cerebellum, "in patients with better cognitive functions (IQ above 60) marked attention deficits, reduced processing speed and visuospatial problems were present" (pp. 237–238). Studies on Turner's syndrome have also implicated the hippocampus and caudate as well as the parieto-occipital system (Murphy, DeCarli, Daly et al. 1993). The more "volumetrically oriented" studies reviewed here create questions about the absoluteness of the "white matter model"; however, it is also true that many genetic disorders *are* associated with white matter functioning such as ADHD (Ashtari, Kumra, Bhaskar, Clarke, Thaden, et al., 2005; Pavuluri, Yang, Kamineni, Passarotti, Srinivasn, et al., 2009) and dyslexia (Deutsch, Dougherty, Bammer, Siok, Gabrieli, & Wandell, 2005; Niogl & McCandliss, 2006).

In terms of neurotransmitter issues, the disorder most heavily studied and for which most support has been found is ADHD (Wilens, 2009). More recently there has been some work finding associations between serotonin and autism (Croonenberghs, Spaas, wauters, Verkerk, Scharpe, et al., 2008; Goldberg, Anderson, Zwaigenbaum, Hall, Nahmias, et al., 2009; Prasad, Steiner, Sutcliffe, & Blakely, 2009), but no investigations related to NVLD specifically. What seems indisputable at this time is that dopamine is implicated in the difficulties children and adults face with ADHD (Madras, Miller, & Fishman, 2005; Potter, Newhouse, & Bucci, 2006; Wilens, 2009). Iversen and Iversen (2007) have a review article spanning the last 50 years looking at what we know about dopamine including not only ADHD but also schizophrenia and Parkinson's disease and its role in these disorders. But dopamine is not the only neurotransmitter implicated in ADHD, there is also a growing body of evidence for a role for norepinephrine (Barton, Mooney, & Prasad, 2005; Geller, Donnelly, Lopez, Rubin, Newcorn, et al., 2007) as well as the central nicotinic cholinergic systems (Potter et al., 2006). At this time, the role of any particular neurotransmitter in the etiology of NVLD does not seem likely. In the future, neurotransmitter issues may become associated with NVLD through disorders that are often linked with NVLD like ADHD (dopamine) or depression (serotonin and norepinephrine).

Environment

Let us look at the first environment of the developing child, the uterus. Not all fetuses develop normally within the uterus. Early birth and/or low birth weight has often been associated with learning disorders. Longitudinal studies in both Canada (Saigal, Szatmari, Rosenbaum, Campbell, & King, 1990) and the Netherlands (Walther, den Ouden, Verloove-Vanhorick, & Pauline, 2000) have established that with a gestational age below 32 weeks and/or birth weight below 1,500 g (a little over 3 lb) this significantly increases the later emergence of developmental disorders with as many as 10% developing severe disabilities. Moreover, learning disorders increased with age in this cohort. The study found that as many as 40% of the children in the study were unable to become fully independent adults (Walther et al., 2000). Even more specific to our topic, these neonatal survivors, although a heterogeneous group in many ways, have at times been found to have a pattern of learning issues similar to NVLD. More specifically "the very low birth weight and extremely low birth weight groups were equivocal to one another in all scores [measures used in the study] except visual perception. The findings also were consistent with a pattern of nonverbal learning disability in which there is evidence of math underachievement and adequate performance in verbal, reading, and spelling scores" (McGrath & Sullivan, 2002, p. 231).

Another disorder potentially associated with NVLD is HIV disease. White matter abnormalities have been associated with a variety of neurobehavioral symptoms with HIV. Brouwers, van der Vlugt, Moss, Wolters, and Pizzo (1995) found deficits in cognitive functioning and socioemotional behavior in children with HIV, concluding that this profile would be in at least partial agreement with Rourke's white matter model of NVLD.

Iatrogenic effects of radiation and chemotherapy on acute lymphoblastic leukemia (ALL) have also, although not consistently, been found to be correlated with an NVLD like disorder among ALL survivors (Moore, Kramer, Wara, Halberg, & Ablin, 1991). Rourke and others have followed up on this research commenting on the neuropsychological consequences of treatment for ALL (Picard & Rourke, 1995) and survivors of pediatric brain tumors (Carey, Barakat, Foley, Gyato, & Phillips, 2001) suggesting that a variety of available treatments have neurotoxicity associated with them which often result in white matter damage and NVLD symptoms. More sophisticated technologies are also being brought to bear on the ALL question. Researchers have found white matter volume decreases utilizing voxel-based morphometry which would also be consistent with Rourke's theory (Carey, Haut, Reminger, Jutter, Theilmann, & Kaemingk, 2008). These data are clearly supportive of environmental events affecting neuropsychological functioning.

Overall, it seems very safe to say that students with NVLD can come by their disabilities via a variety of pathways covering the interaction of genetic, neurobiological, and environmental factors. However, there is a large majority of students who present with an NVLD pattern without a history of a specific genetic disorder or any series of events which logically should eventuate in a nonverbal learning disorder. For instance, a recent study presented at the 2010 American Psychological Association Convention found that when performing structural MRIs on their study participants consisting of Asperger's, NVLD, and control children, one-third of the 28 children with NVLD had cysts or lesions in the occipital region, an area implicated in visuospatial understanding. In stark contrast, only one of the 28 children with Asperger's Disorder and one of the control children had any structural abnormalities (Semrud-Clikeman & Fine, 2011). Clearly, more studies like this are needed to address the etiology of these NVLD types.

White Matter Model

Initially, authors like Semrud-Clikeman & Hynd (1990), Voeller (1986), and Weintraub and Mesulam (1983) conceptualized these nonverbal difficulties as *right hemisphere learning disorders*, all of which (including Rourke's later work) were based on Goldberg, and Costa's (1981) original conceptualizations of how the left and right hemispheres differed in terms of their neuropsychological functions. Denckla (1991) elaborates on this stating "in fact, the frequent association of an attentional/executive functional component and a visuoperceptual/simultaneous information processing component has made the term "right hemisphere LD" seem more appealing in terms of the parsimony afforded by an anatomical expression that captures the affiliation of its behavioral manifestations" (p. 718), although she also cautioned at that time that her conclusion may have been a bit premature.

Moving on from the right hemisphere model, Rourke (1995) postulated that it is more likely that deficits in subcortical white matter are responsible for the symptoms seen in NVLD. Rourke and colleagues (Rourke, 1995; Rourke, Ahmad, Collins, Hayman-Abello, Hayman-Abello, & Warriner, 2002) have written about the neuropsychological symptoms that develop from damage to the white matter, as opposed to gray matter. Hale and Fiorello (2004) describe and have a useful metaphor for the differences between the two. "Recall the central nervous system is primarily composed of gray matter (the nerve cells) and white matter (mylenated axons that speed transformation of information). We like to think of the gray matter as the houses and neighborhoods, and the white matter pathways as the streets and highways" (p. 45). The white matter then is the means by which information is generally transmitted within and between the two hemispheres. As we have learned above from the different genetic disorders that present with NVLD symptoms, these white matter disruptions can be created from a myriad of different causes but ultimately all create somewhat consistent sets of difficulties. To borrow Rourke et al.'s own words (2002):

> The syndrome of NLD [which here is referred to as NVLD] is characterized by significant primary deficits in some dimensions of tactile perception, visual perception, complex psychomotor skills, and in dealing with novel circumstances. These primary deficits lead to secondary deficits in tactile and visual attention and to significant limitations in exploratory behavior. In turn there are tertiary deficits in tactile and visual memory and in concept-formation, problem-solving, and hypothesis-testing skills. Finally, these deficits lead to significant difficulties in the content (meaning) and function (pragmatics) dimensions of language (pp. 310–311).

This approach to understanding has often been referred to as a *cascade* (Schultz, Romanski, & Tsatsanis, 2000) or *downstream* (Fine & Semrud-Clikeman, 2010) effect whereby all the deficits that develop, including some neuropsychological, executive function, academic, linguistic, and social difficulties, are the *result* of the initial or *core* difficulties of tactile perception, visual perception, complex psychomotor skills, and in dealing with novel circumstances. However, here as well, findings can be somewhat inconsistent. For instance, in Wilkinson and Semrud-Clikeman's (2008) study of motor speed in children and adolescents with nonverbal learning disabilities, they found no evidence of tactile perceptual difficulties. As yet we do not have enough consistent empirical support to either endorse or refute the remainder of this theory, but more data are accruing. In addition, as noted above, we are yet to find research which might determine the genetic contribution to the more idiopathic form of NVLD.

Summary

We have offered several ways to understand the varied roads to acquiring NVLD. Such information might allow genetic and/or prenatal counseling, earlier identification and treatment as well as guidance toward the development of targeted interventions. Clinical observation suggests that at this time most NVLD children present without a clear cause of development (idiopathic). Hopefully future studies will offer more definitive answers to these important questions. In the next Chapter (5) we look at the prevalence of NVLD in relationship to gender, SES, and other variables as well as its co- occurrence with other developmental disorders.

Chapter 5
Prevalence and Associated Conditions

This chapter addresses the issues of the incidence, or prevalence, of NVLD in the specific learning-disabled (SLD) and/or clinic populations and known associated conditions. This knowledge can be very important to both policy makers and school personnel as they think about whom they serve and what services are needed. We are looking only at the incidence of NVLD in the SLD or clinic-based populations because those are the only estimates currently available. We will also address the issue of associated conditions in two ways. First, in this chapter we will look at common co-occurring disorders. This issue is typically referred to as *comorbidities*, and in the area of developmental and psychiatric disorders it is often considered more the rule than the exception. Here we are referring to other disorders such as depression, ADHD, the academic disorder, and semantic-pragmatic disorders that are often found co-occurring with NVLD. Second, in the following chapter we will review the available data attempting to look at the relationship between Asperger's Disorder (AS) and NVLD as there remains considerable controversy regarding this issue.

Prevalence

Clinicians and researchers alike lament the lack of epidemiological data on the incidence of NVLD. If we look more generally at the prevalence of *developmental dyscalculia*, a disorder often associated in part with NVLD, it has been estimated that about 5–6% of a school age population meet these criteria (Shalev, 2004). However, not all NVLD students have math disorders and it is clear that math disorders can be created by different processing and intellectual difficulties (Geary, 2000; Marolda & Davidson, 2000). Moving into the clinic or special education populations, on the higher end of the estimate continuum, Johnson (1987a) cited an incidence of about 19% of an adult learning-disordered clinic population could be diagnosed with NVLD. Rourke's (1989) initial estimate of the number of NVLD cases, perhaps the most often cited estimate, among a population of students with specific learning disabilities was 5–10%. However, some of his later findings were a bit different and he and his colleagues suggested that the incidence in a

J.M. Davis and J. Broitman, *Nonverbal Learning Disabilities in Children:*
Bridging the Gap Between Science and Practice, DOI 10.1007/978-1-4419-8213-1_5,
© Springer Science+Business Media, LLC 2011

learning-disabled population could be less than 1% (Casey & Rourke, 1991). This would be somewhat more consistent with Denckla's (1979) earlier estimates of 1% of a learning-disabled population. As we have covered in Chapter 3, NVLD should at this time be considered a *common pathway* disorder and though we do know that the learning-disabled students have an NVLD profile, we are unable to estimate how many of those may be from genetic or environmental causes vs. a more idiopathic form. Clearly, we are unable to arrive at anything definitive at this time; however, Pennington's (2009) notion that estimates for dyslexia and ADHD exceed those of NVLD seems relevant to the current knowledge base. Our clinical experience suggests that approximately 5–10% of the clinic population we see seem to have NVLD profiles. Even though NVLD occurs less frequently than other learning disorders, it is still incumbent upon us as school-based personnel to be able to recognize it and to understand, explain, and intervene appropriately.

Other DSM-IV-TR Comorbidities

Clinicians need to be aware that there are other disorders that often co-occur with NVLD. As we have said before, this is because clinicians need to make sure they are addressing the "big picture" when evaluating children with possible NVLD. Utilizing the heuristic value of the model of NVLD allows us to ensure that we move beyond the "blind men and the elephant" and look at the whole animal to promote full understanding of and interventions for the various symptomotology associated with the disorder. These associated symptoms most often fall into psychiatric, academic, and other developmentally oriented disorders. We will address two of the more prominent psychiatric disorders associated with NVLD: ADHD and depression. We will also review three of the more common academic disorders, which are difficulties with math, reading comprehension, and written expression. Finally, we will review two common comorbid developmental disorders, one of which is in the DSM-IV-TR and is referred to as a Developmental Coordination Disorder (DCD), and the other is a disorder diagnosed primarily by speech and language pathologists and is generally referred to as a semantic–pragmatic disorder.

Psychiatric Disorders

Rourke (1989) reported one of the first and still relevant comorbidities when he noted the presence of ADHD characteristics in NVLD children, especially in their earlier years. In a study by Voeller (1986) of 20 children who met Rourke's criteria for NVLD, all 20 also met criteria for ADHD. The average age of this group was 9.5 years, on the younger side, so it is possible that some of these students would have "outgrown" it, or developed out of it, if they were followed longitudinally. This would clearly fit with the model presented in this book in that a *delay* in early executive function development for NVLD students could produce or mimic ADHD-like symptoms and may help explain Rourke's other finding that many of these younger NVLD children "seem" to outgrow many of these symptoms. Or, within our model, as the executive function system develops, these children can better monitor and/or modulate their motor and attentional systems. So in essence with many NVLD students, their ADHD would be more developmental than a fixed disorder. However, not all NVLD children outgrow their ADHD symptoms and some end up with a comorbid ADHD diagnosis.

Another oft found co-occurring disorder is depression. The question of whether individuals with learning disabilities are more likely to exhibit socioemotional dysfunction than individuals without learning disabilities has been under investigation since at least 1969 (Hallahan & Kaufman, 1976). Review of this literature is complicated by the fact that different investigators studied different aspects of socioemotional dysfunction (e.g., peer rejection vs. clinical depression) and/or used different terms to describe related phenomena (e.g., psychopathology vs. psycho-social adjustment vs. emotional disturbance). In 1989, the *Journal of Learning Disabilities* did a series of articles on possible implications of neuropsychological functioning and suicide and depression (Bigler, 1989). Here Rourke and colleagues (Rourke, Young, & Leenaars, 1989) presented their theory that NVLD predisposes adolescents and adults to depression and suicide and suggest that the issues faced by adolescents and young adults are created by the symptoms of their learning disorder: psychomotor clumsiness, problems with tactile sensitivity, spatial/organi-zational deficits, difficulties with novel situations, and intermodal integration, which then lead to life experiences which they believe are more likely to create despair and depression than other forms of learning disabilities. Research results have been mixed with some finding a reduced Performance IQ relative to Verbal IQ being more associated with childhood and adolescent depression (Brumbach, 1985; Bender, Rosenkrans, & Crane, 1999) while others have not (Mokros, Poznanski, & Merrick, 1989; Forrest, 2004). Historically speaking, there are two common points of view about learning disorders and depression, one articulated by Bruck (1986) and one described by Pearl (1987). Bruck's (1986) review of the available research of the time on socioemotional functioning and learning disabilities reported that there was no clear evidence that children with learning disabilities were signifi-cantly more deviant (in terms of serious behavioral or emotional dysfunction) than children without learning disabilities. On the other hand, children with learning disabilities did appear to have more adjustment problems of a nonclinical nature (e.g., immaturity, being less popular with peers) than children without disabilities. Bruck (1986), however, concluded that these adjustment problems were most likely a result of failure and frustration rather than an integral feature of general learning disabilities. In contrast to Bruck's conclusions Pearl (1987) hypothesized that the same underlying disorder that causes the neurocognitive, linguistic, and academic characteristics of a learning disability also causes the social and emotional features of the disorder much like Rourke. She points out that a longitudinal investigation by Spreen (1988) provided some support for this hypothesis. Spreen classified children with learning disabilities into three groups (definite neurological impairment, suspected neurological impairment, and no neurological impairment) and compared them with a nondisabled control group. He reported that in adulthood, individuals with learning disabilities, and particularly those who had shown clinical signs of neurological impairment in childhood, were more likely to exhibit a variety of socioemotional problems than individuals in the control group.

Little (1993) reviewed all of the available research specifically on NVLD and emotional dysfunction and found that a number of studies provided some degree of support for the hypothesis that individuals with nonverbal learning disabilities are more likely to present with socioemotional dysfunction than individuals with other forms of learning disabilities (or than individuals without learning disabilities). Some of the studies she mentioned are described below. Casey and Rourke (1991), for example, reported overall support for an increase in internalized psychopathology and conduct problems among children with nonverbal learning disabilities between the ages of 7 and 14. Additionally, Weintraub and Mesulam (1983) described 14 individuals with various nonverbal disabilities and heterogeneous neurological impairment but with no indication of dyslexia. These individuals shared a set of emotional difficulties that included disturbed interpersonal skills, social isolation, and chronic depression. In 1986, Rourke, Young, Strang, and Russell reported on eight adults who were referred for serious occupational maladjustment and/or psychiatric problems. Their problems included chronic depression, low self-esteem, loneliness, feelings of isolation, withdrawal, suicide risk, marked difficulty gaining insight in psychotherapy, and (for two of the eight) a diagnosis of schizophrenia. The neuropsychological profiles of all eight individuals indicated good verbal abilities alongside poor nonverbal abilities. Bigler (1989) cited three cases of adult clinic patients who had difficulties with nonverbal processes in addition to depression and suicide risk. Little (1993) makes note that none of these above authors, however, reported comparisons with a nondisabled control group, nor did they provide any indication of how frequently these same symptoms of emotional difficulty appeared in other groups of clinic patients.

At the conclusion of her review, Little (1993) suggests being very cautious about assuming that the link between NVLD and depression is solid and points to numerous problems in the research designs especially lack of control groups and extremely small sample sizes and suggests that the relationship between learning disability subtypes and socioemotional dysfunction is tentative at best and is in need of further investigation. In terms of what we "know" perhaps Pennington (2009) again captures it best when he says: "Because the subjects in all these studies were ascertained clinically, we really do not know what proportion of children with visual-spatial deficits have (and do not have) concomitant social and emotional problems, and what proportion of each of these groups has social and emotional problems as adults" (p. 247).

However it is clinically feasible that children with NVLD difficulties performing many daily life tasks and engaging in many social encounters are very likely to create ongoing stress which could certainly predispose them to heightened emotional issues. Children with AS and NVLD have been described as "perfect victims" when it comes to victimization by their peers because of their profound lack of social skills (Klin, Volkmar, & Sparrow, 2000, p. 6). Liza Little's (2002) survey study found that the overall prevalence rate reported by mothers of children with NVLD and AS was 94%. Mothers reported that almost three-quarters of their children had been hit by peers or siblings in the past year and 75% had been emotionally bullied. On the more severe end of peer victimization, 10% of the children were attacked by a gang in the past year and 15% were victims of nonsexual assaults to the genitals. Peer shunning also was common. A third of the children had not been invited to a single birthday party in the past year, and many were eating alone at lunch or were picked last for teams. Peer shunning was also significantly correlated with peer bullying and assault. Practitioners are well advised to be cognizant of the possibility of presence of depressive affect for any child who has to encounter these potentially socially devastating situations.

Academic Difficulties

There are also the academic disorders classified in the DSM-IV-TR which are often comorbid with NVLD. As noted above, the most prominent in the literature are math problems because having math calculation problems, defined as performance on the Wide Range Achievement Test (1965, 1984), is part of Rourke's (1989, 1995) "definition" of NVLD. However, not all of Rourke's original subjects had math problems, and others have found differing results depending upon the kind of math tasks utilized (Forrest, 2004). In research on math disorders, rather than NVLD subjects, it would seem that there are at least two subtypes (Marolda & Davidson, 2000) and some would argue three subtypes of math disorders (Geary, 2000, 2004) for which the prevalence estimates are about 5–8% of the population. Estimates are that 26% of the 5–8% had comorbid ADHD (Gross-Tsur et al., 1996), 17 over 50% (Badian & Ghubilikian, 1983; Ostad, 1998) comorbid language/reading/ spelling problems, and somewhere around 15–20% of the 5–8% had visual-spatial problems. According to the subtype theorists, and a position with whom we would agree, it is important to ascertain the subtypes so that the interventions can be specific to the needs of the individual child.

   Reading disorders for students with NVLD are very different from those with dyslexia. Although Rourke (1989, 1995) reports that NVLD children can present with early reading problems, most likely due to initial alphabetic learning demands, their reading skills increase dramatically once the symbols are over learned, as opposed to their more phonologically challenged dyslexic peers. However, reading comprehension problems can become problematic for them later in their academic careers (Matte & Bolaski, 1998; Thompson, 1997). Some of the novel problem-solving and inferential difficulties experienced by the NVLD students can interfere with their ability to comprehend some of the more inferential (Worling, Humphries, & Tannock, 1999) or metaphoric (Rourke & Tsatsanis, 1996) kinds of reading comprehension demands as they climb the academic ladder which Palombo (2006) postulates are likely related to the "level of semantic and conceptual processing" demands of those types of questions. As clinicians, we can also see that "knowing" these developmental variations can allow us to "predict" possible difficulties so that parents and school personnel can monitor for them throughout the students' career.

Disorders of written expression, also known as dysgraphia, are also associated with NVLD (Deuel, 1995). And, from a neuropsychological perspective, most consider written language to be the most difficult of the academic skills (Lerner, 2003). Berninger (Berninger & Richards, 2002) has postulated that disorders of written expression are likely to be the most prevalent of the learning disorders, with estimates ranging from 4 to 17% (Hooper, Montgomery, Swartz, Reed, Sandler, et al., 1994). Deuel (1995) describes three types of dysgraphia: dyslexic dysgraphia, motor dysgraphia, and spatial dysgraphia. A quick overview of the subtests would be that *dyslexic dysgraphia* is characterized by poor spelling, both oral and written, but drawing and copying of written tests are generally adequate. For *motor dysgraphia* copied text and spontaneously written productions are problematic and drawing can be problematic, but oral spelling is generally adequate. And with *spatial dysgraphia*, oral spelling is again adequate with problems with drawing and spatial processing. However, estimates by subtype of dysgraphia are not available. It seems reasonable to the authors that there may be some overlaps between the *motor* and *spatial* subtypes with NVLD given the overlapping of symptoms. How these relate to handwriting instruction has often been asked. One of the authors (Davis) recalls a discussion with Virginia Berninger where she stated that for some of these students handwriting instruction is not the answer. She suggested that this sometimes leads to two dysfluent writing systems, printing and cursive, and that for many of these children, working on printing fluency and transferring directly to keyboarding in late elementary or early middle school works more efficiently. The authors are sure that many of us know students we had spent many months on *Handwriting Without Tears* only to have the students resort back to spontaneous printing by middle school.

Other Disorders

DCD, sometimes referred to as developmental dyspraxia, is also estimated to effect about 6% of the school age population (American Psychiatric Association, 2000). Issues noted with early motor developmental milestones, clumsiness, and difficulties with sports and handwriting would all be moderately consistent with aspects of NVLD. In Rourke's (1989, 1995) original model for NVLD, "simple motor" acts were considered to be a primary neuropsychological strength, while "tactile perception" and "complex psychomotor" were primary neuropsychological deficits. However, telling the simple apart from the complex may sometimes be more difficult. For instance, Landau, Auerback, Gross-Tsur, and Shalev (2003) found that a "simple" Finger Tapping Test was significantly slower for NVLD subjects than either ADHD or control subjects. But data such as these do not always replicate consistently.

For example, research on pegboard tasks has at times been found to be more difficult for subjects with NVLD than subjects without NVLD (Durand, Hulme, Larkin, & Snowling 2005; Harnadek & Rourke, 1994), whereas other researchers have not found this to be true Wilkinson & Semrud-Clikeman, (2008). Also, somewhat consistent with the Deuel (1995) model of dysgraphia, recent data have also found subtypes of DCD (Vaivre-Douret, Lalanne, Mouchel, Ingster-Motati, Boddaert, et al., in press). Their model is characterized as having two patterns of DCD, ideomotor and visual spatial, and a third global DCD with multiple comorbidities. If DCD becomes a comorbid condition, typically occupational therapists are brought into the treatment plan/IEP.

Finally, speech and language pathologists also can become primary interveners with NVLD students. Using their nomenclature, these students are most often diagnosed with pragmatic language impairment or semantic pragmatic disorder (Bishop, 2000; Volden, 2004). These types of issues could also underlie some of the reading comprehension problems these students face as well as difficulties with analogical problem solving (Schiff, Bauminger, & Toledo, 2009) and would also be somewhat consistent with current left and right hemisphere traumatic brain injury research, e.g., Bryan and Hale (2001). These issues could also interfere with the understanding of idioms or metaphors in conversation (Rourke, 1995; Worling et al., 1999) which could then also compromise social discourse which is another area speech and language pathologists can focus on in treatment.

Summary

Clearly there are significant overlaps among all of these disorders. Whether we will attempt to address them as subtypes, comorbidities, lines of development, or completely separated disorders is still unclear and only further well-designed research will be able to sort it out. Yet, as clinicians we still need to understand, help others understand, and plan interventions for these clients as best we can. What the authors hope to convey here is that we do have some data that point us in certain ways which we should explore, know about, and help guide clinical decisions. At the same time we suggest caution as there is a great deal we do not yet know about and that we have to be careful about how we explain a client's issues and what we recommend is done about them. In Chapter 6 we will directly address the controversy regarding AS and NVLD. Issues to be considered include whether or not AS and NVLD represent the same disorder with differing levels of severity. Or are they the same disorder. We however, believe they are two different disorder named by two different systems?

Chapter 6
Asperger's Disorder and NVLD

In this chapter we will review available data attempting to look at the relationship between Asperger's Disorder (AS) and NVLD as there remains considerable controversy regarding the relationship, or lack thereof, between these disorders. Some, for example, postulate that they are virtually the same disorder assessed by two different systems: psychiatric evaluations and neuropsychological evaluations, respectively (Klin, Sparrow, Volkmar, Cicchetti, & Rourke, 1995; Volkmar & Klin, 1998). However, other researchers believe that AS is high functioning autism (HFA) and should be considered part of the autistic spectrum (Lord & Spence, 2006; Schopler, 1996), as part of the pervasive developmental disorder spectrum (Szatmari, 1998), or as schizoid-schizotypal disorders (Wolff, 1995). We believe these diagnostic concerns are important not just for the sake of diagnosis but because they will enable us to understand how to intervene with the differing disorders as well.

Research

Historically, Asperger's Disorder was late in arriving to the English-speaking world. Although Hans Asperger originally published his description of what was to become known as Asperger's Disorder in Germany in 1944, the year after Leo Kanner published his description of autism; it was not until 1981 that Lorna Wing published an English account of what Asperger had found. And, it was not until 1994 that Asperger's Disorder was included in the Diagnostic and Statistical Manual of Mental Disorders: 4th edition (DSM-IV-TR). In DSM-IV-TR it is considered a pervasive developmental disorder and is characterized by impairment in social interaction and restricted repetitive and stereotyped patterns of behavior and/or interests. In the DSM-IV-TR it appears as our Table 6.1.

As with most of the DSM-IV-TR disorders, the AS diagnosis is based on behavioral criteria. In contrast with Rourke's criteria for NVLD as listed in Chapter 2, AS diagnosis appears to be different. As mentioned earlier, Asperger's Disorder (AD), also referred to as Asperger's syndrome (AS), is diagnosed from a *psychiatric* perspective, while NVLD is diagnosed from *neuropsychological* perspective.

J.M. Davis and J. Broitman, *Nonverbal Learning Disabilities in Children:* *Bridging the Gap Between Science and Practice*, DOI 10.1007/978-1-4419-8213-1_6,
© Springer Science+Business Media, LLC 2011

Table 6.1 DSM-IV-TR: 299.80 diagnostic criteria for Asperger's Disorder

A. Qualitative impairment is social interaction, as manifested by at least two of the following:
  (1) Marked impairment in the use of multiple nonverbal behaviors such as eye-to-eye gaze, facial expression, body postures, and gestures to regulate social interaction
  (2) Failure to develop peer relationships appropriate to developmental level
  (3) A lack of spontaneous seeking to share enjoyment, interests, or achievements with other people (e.g., by a lack of showing, bringing, or pointing out objects of interest to other people)
  (4) Lack of social or emotional reciprocity
B. Restricted repetitive and stereotyped patterns of behavior, interests, and activities, as manifested by at least one of the following:
  (1) Encompassing preoccupation with one or more stereotyped and restricted patterns of interests that are abnormal either in intensity or focus
  (2) Apparently inflexible adherence to specific, nonfunctional routines or rituals
  (3) Stereotyped and repetitive motor mannerisms (e.g., hand or finger flapping or twisting, or complex whole-body movements)
  (4) Persistent preoccupation with parts of objects
C. The disturbance causes clinically significant impairment on social, occupational, or other important areas of functioning
D. There is no clinically significant general delay in language (e.g., single words used by age 2 years, communicative phrases used by age 3 years)
E. There is no clinically significant delay in cognitive development or in the development of age-appropriate self-help skills, adaptive behavior (other than in social interaction), and curiosity about the environment in childhood
F. Criteria are not met for another specific pervasive developmental disorder or Schizophrenia

(American Psychiatric Association 2000, p. 84)

Although Rourke talks about the types of social difficulties NVLD children and adolescents often face, he postulates that the behavioral problems seen in those with NVLD, such as issues with social judgment, misperception of feelings/expressions of others, lack of prosody, and difficulty with adaptability to novel interpersonal situations, are the result of the primary neuropsychological problems they have with tactile perception, visual perception, and complex psychomotor functions.

In collaboration with Klin, Volkmar, Sparrow, and Cicchetti (1995), Rourke considered the similarities between NVLD and AS. Twenty-one persons diagnosed with AS (average age 16.11) with 19 persons diagnosed with HFA (average age 15.36) recruited from clinical populations were compared. The authors found that 18 of the 21 AS persons presented with NVLD profiles while only 1 of the 19 HFA persons presented more with an NVLD profile. However, as Szatmari (1998) has pointed out, the Klin et al. (1995) group included motor clumsiness as one of the symptoms for AS (Gilberg, 1991). This means that through the selection criteria for the study it selected a symptom that then became one of its findings. This alone, he suggests, could have influenced the extent of visual motor involvement in their AS group. Previous studies (Ghaziuddin, Butler, Tsai, & Ghaziuddin, 1994; Marjiviona & Prior, 1995) had not found motor clumsiness any more frequently among AS children when compared to those diagnosed with autism.

Tony Attwood (2007), another leading authority on AS, stated in his most recent book that "A similar discrepancy between Verbal IQ and Performance IQ for children with Asperger's syndrome has now been confirmed by several studies. Children with a much higher Verbal IQ and Performance IQ and a particular profile of cognitive abilities are described as having Non-Verbal Learning Disability or NLD" (p. 230). However, if we actually review the studies cited, we learn that Attwood's conclusion is only partially accurate. For instance, Ghaziuddin and Mountain-Kinchi (2004) reported that AS subjects had higher Verbal IQs than autistic subjects and that AS subjects did have a significantly lower Performance IQ. However, if we look more closely at the performance subtests of the WISC-III on which the AS subjects performed relatively more poorly, Picture Arrangement and Coding, we find that these subtests may not be the best measures of spatial ability. According to the Bannatyne (1974) factors, it was the Block Design, Object Assembly, and Picture Completion scores which cluster into the "spatial" reasoning factor, not Picture Arrangement or Coding, which are more often thought to demand understanding of social situations (Picture Arrangement) and fine motor efficiency (Coding). Unfortunately, with Klin et al.'s (1995) study, the subtest scores were not available.

In a similar vein, Cederlund and Gillberg (2004), using the Gillberg criteria (1991), looked at a retrospective study of 100 males with AS from their medical records. Here they found that only 51% of AS subjects met criteria for NVLD much lower than the Klin et al. findings. Also, again Coding was the most salient subtest and again using the Bannatyne criteria, the differences between verbal and spatial reasoning were not as compelling. In yet another study of the cognitive profiles of 37 children and adolescents with AS *not* utilizing the Gillberg criteria by Barnhill, Hagiwara, Myles, and Simpson (2000), the difference between VIQ and PIQ was *not* statistically different, however the Coding subtest was the lowest score on the performance subtests. Finally, in a more recent study comparing AS, NVLD, ADHD, and controls (using DSM-IV criteria for the AS and ADHD groups), the NVLD group did do more poorly on PIQ than the AS group using the Wechsler Abbreviated Intelligence Scales (WASI: Semrud-Clikeman, in press). What is very interesting is that WASI only includes the Block Design and Matrix Reasoning subtests, not Coding or Picture Arrangement. Future studies will need to address whether AS and NVLD *are* as similar as some suggest, or whether in fact the differences are in *primarily* fine motor issues and/or social perception issues, as Gillberg suggests (1991). While researchers will no doubt continue working to resolve this issue, clinicians have formulated impressions based on case-by-case experiences with persons diagnosed with AS and NVLD.

Clinical Perspectives

Among clinicians there is much discussion regarding the "experienced differences" and similarities between children with AS and children with NVLD. However, both the research and clinical issues are further complicated by the possibility that there are subtypes of NVLD and that all children with AS do not present exactly alike or may also be composed of subtypes. Not all children with the NVLD profile will, for example, exhibit social deficits (Pennington 1991). There is however a great deal of clinical anecdotal information supporting the idea that the child with NVLD and the child with AS "feels" very different in your office (Palombo, 2006). Forrest (2004) claims that the main difference between the two disorders, as they are most frequently defined clinically, is the absence in children with NVLD of restricted interests or special skills. Little (2003) notes that the child with AS is considered by many clinicians to present with more serious social deficits than the child with NVLD. Indeed, some suggest that AS may be a more severe variant of NVLD (Brumback, Harper, Warren, & Weinberg, 1996; Volkmar & Klin, 1998). Fast (2004) believes that children with NVLD have normal emotions but are inept in expressing them and in recognizing them in others, to the extent that they are expressed nonverbally. She finds that children with AS, on the other hand, do not feel the normal range of emotions, have a flat affect, and have difficulty with initiating or experiencing normal social relationships. Most clinicians agree that children with Asperger's have greater social problems and more severely odd behaviors beyond what is usually seen in children with NVLD (Mamen, 2007). The highly restricted interests of the AS children appear to present an additional obstacle to their social functioning. Contrary to Klin et al. (1995), Fast (2004) also notes that children with AS in her practice do not appear to have problems with visual-spatial issues, which are a major problem area for most children with NVLD. In fact, she finds that many of the children with AS that she has seen respond well to visuals and diagrams and are "visual learners." She reports that many find work as engineers or architects. In contrast, the children with NVLD from her practice do not respond to physical demonstrations and may not understand diagrams. They do not learn as well from demonstrations and need everything explained in words. Fast (2004) finds that many adults with NVLD tend to become "wordsmiths" such as teachers and writers, while adults with AS often excel in math and find work in computer fields.

Mamen (2007) offers the following list of characteristics from her clinical experience of children with Asperger's but not found in children with NVLD:

- Indifference to peer contacts
- Indifference to feelings of others
- Lack of spontaneous sharing of enjoyment
- Narrow, exclusive, abnormal interests
- Inflexible adherence to nonfunctional routines
- Stereotypic motor mannerisms
- Persistent preoccupation with parts of objects
- Delayed speech development
- Idiosyncratic use of words
- Repetitive speech patterns
- Noncommunicative
- Clinically significant early language delays
- Clinically significant cognitive delays

An occupational therapist, Rondalyn Whitney, offers the following descriptions on the Lighthouse (a treatment center for autistic spectrum children and adults) Website (http://www.thelighthouseproject.com/Difference%20between%20NLD %20and%20AS.htm) of two twin males from her practice, one diagnosed with NVLD and the other with AS, to help highlight what she perceives as clinical differences between adults with the two disorders.

I know a set of adult twins, one of whom has NLD and one who has Asperger's. In some ways, they could be the same person, but in other ways, it's obvious how different NLD and AS really are. A prime example is their pantry. Tom has a poor visual memory, so he can never remember (except in the most general sense) where stuff goes when he has to put it back. If stuff gets back on the same shelf after he's done cooking, he's a happy boy (even if it isn't particularly neat). Kyle, on the other hand, is an arranger. His particular compulsion has to do with the pantry. Tom drives Kyle crazy, because he never puts stuff away where it "belongs." Kyle has a fit when Tom puts the groceries away. At least once a week, Kyle goes through the pantry and puts everything in its spot, perfectly aligned. Even when the rest of the house and especially the bedroom is a disaster, the pantry is tidy as a display case.

While Kyle has to force himself to put something in the same spot every day so Kyle can remember where he put it, he has invariant places where stuff MUST go. His tennis shoes are always in exactly the same spot under the coffee table, every day. It drives Tom crazy, but if Tom moves them, they just find their way back. He remembers the exact location of a number of objects and likes them in a certain spot – Tom has learned not to move them, even if he doesn't like where they are (enough times getting growled out for "spiriting away" his stuff). Tom can't even remember where he left his keys half the time and wouldn't notice if someone moved them!

The sense of direction is another big difference. Kyle has one. A great one. It took him two days to learn his way around town (and he loves to look at maps). Tom still can't figure out where he is half the time. And Kyle can't figure out how on earth Tom could NOT have a sense of direction, that lack of ability to take the perspective of another and understand that what is in his brain isn't automatically in Tom's brain.

Their reading habits are totally different, too, though they both like science fiction. One of Kyle's big obsessions is Star Wars (he can repeat every movie, along with the movie, word for word!), and he must read all the books, regardless of whether he likes them or not. If Tom doesn't like a book, Tom usually ends up reading about 30 pages of it and putting it aside. Kyle will grumble the whole time, but he ALWAYS finishes the book. Kyle has a terrible time remembering books he just read – but he can quote some passages verbatim months later! And he likes nonfiction primarily about architecture and building, manners, and education. …

In the area of social, both children with NLD and AS have difficulty understanding the perspective of another person but when taught that perspective, children with NLD seem to recall what they've learned and apply it more often and more effectively. Children with AS seem to need more repetition of the social concepts and more practice in the application of those concepts. Children with NLD more commonly want to belong and be a part of groups or in relationship with peers so badly that they have a tendency to be annoying and overbearing in their overtures. People with AS tend to be more aloof, more content with one or two friends and tend to be more withdrawn or isolated. One of the diagnostic criteria for NLD is tactile imperceptions, that is they have trouble recognizing objects placed in their hands with their eyes occlude and have difficulty identifying letters drawn on their fingers with eyes occluded. In my clinical experience, I have not found this to be true with the children with AS but it is always true in the children with NLD.

Finally to further fill out aspects of the *clinical* picture of the differences between AS and NVLD we offer parent advocate Larry Blim's (2002) list of nine experiential ways in which a child with AS is different from a child with NVLD. Blim finds that regarding AS:

1. It affects boys much more than girls.
2. It may be characterized by restricted and unusual patterns of interest and behavior which can be very unsettling to parents.
3. The speech of kids with Asperger's may be fact-based and fact-obsessed and the child with Asperger's may be unable to understand or engage in the nuances of normal conversation. Or even notice that such nuances exist.
4. Kids with AS may have bizarre fixations such as memorizing the birthdays of every member of Congress.
5. Kids with Asperger's may engage in preservative scripting, such as memorizing entire TV shows and reciting them over and over.
6. Children with Asperger's may be characterized by monotonic speech, social isolation, and a paucity of empathy.
7. Children with Asperger's can exhibit regular temper tantrums and erratic behavior such as rolling on the floor (to see what it feels like) or rocking incessantly, or they might engage in self-stimulation like holding their hands together and jumping up and down – and have no idea that such behaviors are inappropriate. (Authors note: He is referring to elementary school-age children here and older, not toddlers.)
8. Their social interactions are not merely inept; they tend to be disastrous, because their language tends to be both insular and rigid. They may not only lack social graces, but also have to be taught them by rote. They may have no intuition for social interaction, and may, for example, use memorized dialog from a movie in a conversation with another person. This might occur whether the other person has seen that movie or not. If you ask a kid with Asperger's how he is, he might respond "Why do you want to know?"
9. Kids with Asperger's may have trouble with the imaginary logic, for example, activities such as fire drills; one child got time out because he refused to participate in fire drills since there was no actual fire. His refusal stemmed less from defiance than from an inability to understand why anyone would want to pretend that there was a fire. Another child was asked to pretend that he had no homework, and then was angry because he had to do the homework which in his mind did not exist.

Summary

In this chapter we describe the origin of Asperger's disorder and its behavioral criteria for inclusion in DSM-IV-TR. We have also reviewed both the research and clinical data looking at the evidence and arguments about whether AS and NVLD are actually the same disorder from two differing perspectives: psychiatric and neuropsychological. We found that one of the major problems with the research in this area was the lack of consistent inclusion criteria for selection for the clinical groups (see for instance Fine, Semrud-Clikeman, Bledsoe, & Hasson's meta-analysis of NVLD research, 2010). It seems clear that the question of the relation between children with NVLD and children with AS needs additional research. Future studies that attempt to understand any similarities or differences between AS and NVLD might investigate a variety of cognitive, affective, behavioral, and social differences. Two centers currently at work on aspects of this are Rush Neurobehavioral Center in Chicago and the Center for Neurodevelopmental Studies at Michigan State University. We eagerly await their results. In Chapter 7, we discuss eligibility for special services.

Chapter 7
Eligibility for Special Services, Screening, and Assessment

This chapter will cover eligibility for special services including brief overviews of both the Individuals with Disabilities Education Act-2004 and Section 504 of the Rehabilitation Act of 1973. Since our model suggests that students with NVLD often have academic and social impairment, knowing the pertinent laws will help the students and their families get the added support they will need.

Eligibility: Specific Learning Disability

Practitioners will frequently have to help their clients/students with NVLD determine if they are eligible to receive special services within the public school system. Therefore, it is important to understand that there are two main federal laws available to practitioners to help get these students special interventions and/or accommodations. The first to be discussed is the Individuals with Disabilities Education Act-2004 (IDEA-04) and its various incarnations. This act started with PL 94-142 in 1975 which set the stage for the definition for a learning disability. The second is Section 504 from the Rehabilitation Act of 1973, often referred to as the "level the playing field" law as it initially was set up to provide handicapped access to buildings. Although many private schools these days will provide accommodations for children, they have no *mandated services*, leaving students subject to the individual school's discretion.

IDEA-04

For those of our students who are significantly struggling with academics or socio-emotional functioning, the original law establishing the existence of a "specific learning disability" and a severe emotional disturbance was PL 94-142, or the Education for All Handicapped Children Act of 1975. Although modified along the way, the basic definition of a learning disability has remained the same in IDEA-04

J.M. Davis and J. Broitman, *Nonverbal Learning Disabilities in Children:*
Bridging the Gap Between Science and Practice, DOI 10.1007/978-1-4419-8213-1_7,
© Springer Science+Business Media, LLC 2011

as it was in the 1975. For students with NVLD and academic difficulties, IDEA-04 addresses eligibility for special education by designating them as a child with a specific learning disability (SLD). To meet consideration for a SLD, the following criteria must be met:

1. Low achievement in one of eight specified areas:

   (a) Oral expression
   (b) Listening comprehension
   (c) Written expression
   (d) Basic reading skill
   (e) Reading fluency skills
   (f) Reading comprehension
   (g) Mathematics calculation
   (h) Mathematics problem solving

2. Using either (a) an RTI approach whereby the child does not meet academic expectations given an evidence-based teaching program or (b) pattern of strengths and weaknesses and/or discrepancy model approach to identify children who may have a specific learning disability. This looks for a case where there is a significant discrepancy between aptitude, usually a measure of IQ, and achievement, usually taken to be a standardized measure of academic achievement in one or more of the above areas, along with the coexistence of a processing disorder (e.g., visual-spatial processing) which is presumed to be the central cause of the discrepancy

3. The exclusionary factors approach, which requires that the disability is not due to sensory impairment, lack of school attendance, emotional disturbance, an intellectual disability, or any environmental, cultural, or economic disadvantage [Section 300.8 (c) (10) of the IDEIA Code of Federal Regulations (CFR), p. 46551]. IDEA-04 newly addresses the need to assure that the child has had appropriate instruction, and that with intervention progress has to be documented, e.g., the achievement gap between the SLD student and the non-SLD student has to narrow. Remaining perpetually behind, theoretically, is no longer an option. Each state has the option of choosing which model they will use to document a learning disability, but some states have left it to the individual school districts to decide (Yell, 2006). If the above conditions are believed to have been met without success utilizing the more traditional SLD diagnostic, the child then needs to be referred for a comprehensive psychoeducational evaluation. This will then determine if he or she qualifies as a child with a specific learning disability who needs special education.

If an RTI approach to instruction and intervention is utilized, it works somewhat differently. This approach has been brought to the prominent attention of educators due to being referenced in IDEA-04. RTI refers to the practice of providing "high quality instruction and interventions matched to student need, monitoring progress frequently to make decisions about changes in instruction or goals and applying child response data to important educational decisions" (Griffiths, Parson, Burns, VanDerHeyden, & Tilly, 2007 p. 3). In schools where an RTI model has been implemented, a tiered system of interventions is provided to students identified as either not meeting early benchmarks or not making expected levels of progress as a result of an intervention targeting a specified academic deficit. For our NVLD population this would most typically be math. However, it is also clear that the RTI model is best developed for reading relative to other academic areas (see for instance Fletcher-Janzen & Reynolds, 2008). Within this model, a lack of response to high-quality instruction or intervention that works for most students indicates the need for a more intensive or broader intervention. If sufficient progress is not then made, that is likely to lead to a comprehensive evaluation and special education consideration. The U.S. Department of Education's (2007) Office of Special Education Programs (OSEP) has stated that using the RTI model does not replace a comprehensive evaluation but can be part of the comprehensive evaluation if the interventions do not work.

RTI approaches are referred to in IDEA-04 as one process for determining whether a child should be referred for a comprehensive evaluation to determine need and eligibility (U.S. Department of Education, 2006, 34 CFR § 300.309[a] [2]) for special education services as a student with a specific learning disability. RTI approaches rest on two solid research bases: (a) findings supporting the effectiveness of early intervening for children experiencing delays in reading development and (b) findings regarding the usefulness of formative progress monitoring of key academic skills. Although the results of an RTI process do not determine eligibility for special education services, as argued nicely by Fletcher-Janzen and Reynolds (2008), the data gathered during an RTI process should play an important part in a comprehensive evaluation.

Common features of RTI models include the following: high-quality, evidence-based instruction and intervention, methods for assuring fidelity in the implementation of interventions, universal screening of all children to identify those at risk of academic problems, early intervention, and progress monitoring of students receiving intervention services (Bender & Shores, 2007; Fuchs & Fuchs, 2006; Mellard & Johnson, 2007; NASDSE, 2007). An RTI model provides a framework for a tiered approach to providing interventions of varying levels of intensity to struggling students. These models may have from three to five levels of interventions. Within the most typical three-tiered RTI model, the first tier represents classroom instruction.

The RTI model assumes that the classroom curriculum is effective for most students and that within the curriculum there are methods for differentiating the instruction according to student need. The second tier consists of more intensive interventions for those students not responding appropriately to first tier instruction. Intensity can be increased through smaller instructional groups, more focused instruction (possibly with a supplemental program), or more instructional time. However, this second tier of intervention is still considered to be within the regular educational system, not part of special education. In some models the third tier represents the types of interventions that are more typical of special education and are characterized by greater intensity of instruction achieved through individualized focus, remedial curriculum, or more time.

Data that can be expected to result from an RTI approach consist at a minimum of information on what specific instructional methods and intervention strategies were used. In addition, one might learn how effective these methods were with other students, and how the student is progressing on key academic indicators of literacy. Lastly, we should learn where the student performs in relation to his or her peers, and the amount of progress that he or she displays in response to the instruction and intervention utilized. The RTI process provides valuable information about the student's instructional history, which is useful both in eligibility decisions and in future educational planning, but never dictates the actual instruction that is to take place; this is one of the criticisms often leveled at the RTI model (Hale, Naglieri, Kaufman, & Kavale, 2004). In addition, diagnostic information (such as behavior rating scales and phonological processing measures) may have been collected as a result of failure to respond and this information will also become part of the comprehensive evaluation. It is beyond the scope of this chapter to discuss RTI models in depth; however, for further more information, the reader is referred to http://www.nrcld.org/topics/rti.html and/or the *Handbook of Response to Intervention* (Jimerson, Burns, & VanDerHeyden, 2007).

Eligibility: Seriously Emotionally Disturbed

If our student with NVLD is struggling more with socioemotional issues, the eligibility criteria for the seriously emotionally disturbed (SED) category may be more helpful to that child. Federal law has changed the eligibility category from SED to "emotionally disturbed" (ED), although the terms are still often used interchangeably. The criteria in both state and federal law have remained the same. A student meets criteria for SED if, *because of a serious emotional disturbance,*[1] he or she exhibits one or more of the following characteristics, over a long period of time, and to a marked degree *and* the student's SED adversely affects his or her educational performance:

1. An inability to learn which cannot be explained by intellectual, sensory, or health factors
2. An inability to build or maintain satisfactory interpersonal relationships with peers and teachers
3. Inappropriate types of behavior or feelings under normal circumstances exhibited in several situations
4. A general pervasive mood of unhappiness or depression
5. A tendency to develop physical symptoms or fears associated with personal or school problems [34 C.F.R. Sec. 300.7(c) (4); 5 C.C.R. Sec. 3030(i)]

---

[1] Note that this phrase is only included in the state definition.

SED as a category of special education was created by Congress and is not associated with any specific psychiatric diagnosis. This means that to be found SED does not require any specific psychiatric diagnosis as might be found in DSM-IV-TR (2000). A student does not need to have a psychiatric diagnosis to be eligible under federal and state definitions of SED. However, federal regulations do require that the characteristics enumerated above be caused by a "serious emotional disturbance" and specifically excludes students whose behaviors are caused by "social maladjustment," which unfortunately, the regulations do not define. Given this situation, there has been a lack of clarity as to what conditions qualify as a student for the SED category, and what conditions are to be considered "social maladjustment" which would not qualify the student for SED services.

Section 504

Since some students with NVLD can do well enough academically such that they are not eligible for IDEA-2004 criteria, Section 504 legislation is another vehicle from which we may be able to provide support to our students. 504 plans may also be useful for students who although eligible for IEPs prefer to remain mainstreamed. The team might also decide for clinical reasons that a 504 plan is the option of choise. Section 504 has its history in civil rights legislation. It was introduced in Congress and ratified in 1973. Fundamentally, it prohibits discrimination against individuals with disabilities. It is meant to ensure that a student with a disability has equal access to an education, and is often referred to as the "level the playing field" law. The child may receive accommodations and modifications to his or her educational program so that his or her disability does not prevent the student from being able to achieve. Also, effective January 1, 2009, the Adults with Disabilities Act (ADA) changed to emphasize that the definition of a disability should be understood as in favor of broad coverage of individuals to the maximum extent permitted by the terms of the ADA. Section 504 was also amended so that it now incorporates the revised ADA by reference as it applies to public school students under Section 504. This is useful not only for receiving help, but is also relevant to those students who move on to college after their K-12 career, as college and/or university criteria for special accommodations take place under ADA.

Unlike IDEA-04, Section 504 does not require the school to provide an individualized educational program (IEP) that is designed to meet the child's unique needs and to provide the child with services which are to have an educational benefit. Also, under Section 504, fewer procedural safeguards are available to children with disabilities and their parents than under IDEA-04. However, a Section 504 Plan must be developed by the Section 504 team if the student meets the criteria of having a disability that creates a "functional impairment" which creates a problem for the student to access the school or institution's standard curriculum. The team must meet annually to reevaluate the status of the plan to insure that the student has every possible chance to participate fully in the educational process. Depending upon the disability, which might apply to both a student with a learning disorder and a student with severe emotional problems, the functional impairment criteria can sometimes be a bit amorphous.

The focus here, as in most parts of this book, is that we need to understand the child's strengths and weaknesses and the impact of these strengths and weaknesses on life in and out of school. With this clinical knowledge we can then proceed to the next step, which is figuring out clinically what the student will need to be successful. After establishing this, we can then see which set of laws governing helping children in the schools is most appropriate for getting the child the support he or she needs and also in terms of what the targets will be for the intervention and accommodations which will be included in the IEP and/or Section 504 Plans. To qualify for these services, documentation must be provided. The data used for documentation can come from private practice practitioners or school-based practitioners. The next chapter will present methods of screening and evaluating to obtain the necessary data to present for eligibility decisions and/or for clinical interventions.

Summary

In this chapter we reviewed the two sets of laws for which children with NVLD may qualify for specific intervention or accommodation. These are the Individuals with Disabilities Education Act-2004 and Section 504 of the Rehabilitation Act of 1973. Practitioners need to be familiar with these laws to assure that they help their students receive all possible services. Next in Chapter 8, we will present methods for screening for NVLD, including the Response to Intervention (RTI) model and our model for the comprehensive psychoeducational assessment of NVLD.

Chapter 8
Screening and Evaluation

As we have stated, data are the source for identifying students with NVLD, qualifying students with NVLD, and determining what types of interventions and accommodations will be necessary to help insure their success. Here we will discuss two methods for collecting data: screening and a comprehensive evaluation. Screening can be used for determining with whom to intervene, as in an RTI model, or for determining for whom a broader evaluation is necessary. A broader evaluation is necessary for helping to document eligibility for services (Hale, Nagliari, Kaufman, & Kavale, 2006) and for deciding where, with what professionals, and with what goals the services are to be provided. Screening may well be the first step toward identifying those students who need support.

Screening for NVLD

Screening can be an important way to begin to find students who either are struggling or are likely to struggle. It is also incumbent upon us as school-based personnel, under the child find aspects of IDEA-04 to find and help children who are in need. One of the prominent methods to have been developed recently is Response to Intervention (RTI: Fuchs & Fuchs, 2006: Mellard & Johnson, 2008), but other approaches will also be presented below.

RTI, is well developed for identifying reading difficulties, however, it has begun to be used as a way to screen for math. Since many of our students with NVLD have difficulties with math they may be identified through this process. While the RTI model offers a way to do this, our position is that without further data collection RTI alone would not clarify which of the students having difficulties with math were actually students with NVLD (Feifer, 2008). Searches of Psychinfo and Pubmed yielded only two published articles and one dissertation pertaining to this area confirming that there is little validated and reliable empirical information available to help us screen for NVLD. Both NewDelman (1997) and Williams, Killgore, Glahn, and Casasanto (2005) created screening tools designed for the college level.

NewDelman (1997) developed a questionnaire which she called the NewDelman Assessment of Learning Disabilities (NANoLD). She correlated this new instrument with a variety of instruments (the Spatial Relations subtest of the Woodcock–Johnson-R, the Profile of Nonverbal Sensitivity, the Toronto Alexithymia Scale, and the trait portion of the State-Trait Anxiety Inventory). Correlations were modest but NewDelman concluded that with further study the NANoLD may become an effective tool in identifying college students with NVLD. Williams et al. (2005) developed a brief pencil and paper screener modeled after the WAIS-III: Block Design to quickly assess visuospatial abilities in college students. They called it the Design Organization Test (DOT) and found that it correlated very significantly with the WAIS-III: Block Design subtest ($r = .92$). Further, they concluded that it would be a useful screener for visuospatial problems among college students. In this book, we are focused on the elementary to high school group of students, although one could argue that similar screeners could be developed for younger students.

The work of Cornoldi, Venneri, Marconato, Molin, and Montiari (2003) most directly addresses our population of concern. Originally done in Italy and replicated in England, Cornoldi et al. developed an 18 item questionnaire which translates to English as the *Shortened Visuospatial Questionnaire (SVS)*. The authors explained that they preferred the term *visuospatial learning disability (VSLD)* to the term commonly used here, NVLD, because they wanted to highlight their position that the most salient characteristic of these students is a spatial processing problem.

In the first part of the study they had teachers rate each of their students across the 18 items after receiving information and training on the questionnaire. The scores were totaled and a clinical cutoff score was derived. In a second part of the study, the students were separated into two groups, one with supposed visuospatial processing issues and a control group. These students were then given a brief battery of neuropsychological tests to validate the *SVS*. The authors' state that:

> this twofold validation procedure demonstrated that with the use of an appropriate cutoff, the risks of false positives and false negatives are low. One strong point in the approach to validation in this study is the confirmation by psychometric testing that children rated by the *SVS* questionnaire as having VSLD did indeed show a visuospatial deficit when individually tested for these abilities (p. 305).

The article does have a copy of the screening instrument attached in English, how to score it, and the clinical cutoff scores should any reader be interested in pursuing it further. Further research should prove interesting to see if the *SVS* retains its high level of discrimination. We believe it could be a valuable tool to add to RTI, speech and language, and occupational screening evaluations to see if there is a larger set of issues in need of further evaluation to better understand and develop interventions for our students.

What also needs to be reemphasized here is that NVLD is a complicated disorder. Screening for math alone will not tell us if the student has NVLD. A more comprehensive evaluation will be needed to see if other issues emerge and therefore whether other supports will be needed for the child. In section "Psychoeducational Evaluation: A Critical Component," we will present our model for the comprehensive psychoeducational assessment of NVLD.

Psychoeducational Evaluation: A Critical Component

As Fine and Semrud-Clikeman (2010) have recently stated, given the current empirical knowledge base for NVLD plus the lack of consensus for *what* NVLD is, evaluating for and diagnosing NVLD is problematic (see also Forrest, 2004). Also, there is no consensus on whether there are any core deficits, and questions regarding whether NVLD may share symptoms with both AS (Klin, Volkmar, Sparrow, & Cicchetti, 1996) and ADHD (Hain, Hale, & Glass-Kendorski, 2009), which would then need to be *ruled out* in order to help establish an NVLD diagnosis. We believe that a comprehensive evaluation is needed to establish a diagnosis as well as identify the particular symptoms for a specific child. One must be able to explain and understand what a specific learner's strengths and weaknesses are to decide upon appropriate interventions and to design accommodations and/or scaffolding to better enhance the learner's chance for success. To do this we develop and present a model for assessment.

Our model includes the eight general areas which we believe need to be considered; they are listed in Table 8.1. The reader will see that we are proposing an information-processing approach to understanding the tests and the child's responses to the tests similar to what is generally referred to as the Boston Processing Model (White & Rose, 1997). This model includes the idea that the name of the test you are using may not really reflect what it is measuring, although it may put you into a basic area of processing. Rather, it is the action and/or reaction of the child, observed either by watching the child's performance and/or administering differing subtests, that allows us to better understand the process about which we want to know. Or in other words, it is our position that it is not the number the child receives for any particular test that is important, but rather how the child *obtained* that number. In Table 8.2 we suggest the processing areas of interest which need to be assessed. In addition in Table 8.3 we offer some examples of current tests which could be used to accomplish these goals in the assessment process. This model is predicated on trying to insure that all the information processing and/or neuropsychological processes associated with academic success and which contribute to the process of being an efficient learner are assessed. An alternative model for thinking about how to analyze test data and a much more

Table 8.1 A neurodevelopmental testing framework

- IQ
- Attention and executive functioning
- Learning and memory
- Sensory motor and graphomotor
- Language
- Visual processing
- Affect and behavior
- Academic testing

Table 8.2　Eight areas of essential cognitive functions

IQ	Executive functioning and attention	Memory			Sensory motor	
		Visual	Verbal	Vis/verb integration	Bilateral efficiency	Proprioceptive
Verbal or crystallized	Attention/focus initiation	Real vs. abstract	Contextual vs. decontextual	Real vs. abstract	Simple vs. complex	Pencil grip
Fluid/pattern analysis	Working memory Planning/ organizing internalized	Recognition vs. retrieval Sequential vs. nonsequential	Recognition vs. retrieval Sequential vs. nonsequential	Recognition vs. retrieval	Timed vs. untimed Sequential vs. nonsequential	
Visuospatial Quantitative	Planning/ organizing externalized Self-monitoring Task completion	Immediate vs. working vs. long-term memory	Immediate vs. working vs. long-term memory			

Graphomotor		Language		Visual processing	Affect and behavior
Timed	Untimed	Receptive	Expressive	Sequential vs. nonsequential	Depression Anxiety
Grapho-symbol Grapho-nonsymbol	Design drawing	Phonemic awareness Morphological awareness Syntax Semantics Pragmatics Receptive vocabulary	Rapid naming Expressive vocabulary Verbal fluency	Timed vs. untimed Orthograpic processing	Thought problems Social problems Oppositional conduct Self-esteem

Academic testing		
Math	Reading	Writing
Math concepts Math calculation Math application Math fluency	Basic word reading Non- or psuedoword reading Reading fluency Reading comprehension: literal and figurative/inferential	Spelling Writing basics: punctuation, capitalization, grammar Writing fluency Sentence writing Paragraph composition Narrative Expository

exhaustive list of tests can be found in *Essentials of Cross Battery Assessment: Second Edition* (Flanagan, Ortiz, & Alfonso, 2007).

In the following sections, we describe each of the eight areas in detail and offer sample test options for assessing each of the skill sets. The tests mentioned below are selected based on our clinical experience. Unfortunately, here, as in many places, there is yet to be empirical literature describing which tests are most sensitive to identifying NVLD generated. We believe that multiple areas of assessment are needed.

Intellectual Assessment

We are not particularly interested in the number associated by a full scale IQ score. However, we are suggesting that there are four areas of cognitive functioning/reasoning that we believe are best measured by IQ tests such as the WISC-IV, DAS-II, KABC-II, and Stanford–Binet-V, that are critical to assess. They are *verbal reasoning and comprehension, perceptual reasoning, fluid reasoning, and quantitative reasoning.* We will describe each of them.

By *verbal reasoning* we mean the ability to reason or think with words. This is also sometimes referred to as semantic reasoning. Our battery is Wechsler-focused so we typically use the Wechsler Intelligence Scale for Children – 4th edition: Verbal Comprehension Index (WISC-IV: VCI: Wechsler, 2003) for this, although all other measures of intellectual reasoning do assess this area. Verbal intelligence has been documented many times to be a relative strength for children with NVLD (for instance, see Rourke, 1995; Semrud-Clikeman, Fine, & Bledsoe, 2008b).

By *perceptual reasoning* we mean the ability to think and/or reason nonverbally, in pictures, geometric designs, especially spatial reasoning, etc. Perceptual or visuospatial reasoning would be a relative deficit for NVLD children (Rourke, 1995; Semrud-Clikeman, Walkowiak, Wilkinson, & Christopher, 2010). In a recent study utilizing the WISC-IV, Hain (2008) found that the two most affected scores for students with NVLD were the Block Design and Symbol Search subtests, Block Design being one of the core subtests for the WISC-IV: PRI. We believe this to be especially important for students with possible NVLD because we agree with Cornoldi et al. (2003) that visual-spatial concerns are of critical interest for students with NVLD, and our subtype model suggests this focus as well. We usually measure this via the WISC-IV: PRI, but with caution. As Keith et al. (2006) found in their refactoring of the WISC-IV standardization data, the PRI can really be broken down into two factors, a spatial reasoning factor (Block Design and Picture Completion) and a fluid reasoning factor (Picture Concepts and Matrix Reasoning). We also frequently use the Wide Range Assessment of Visual Motor Abilities: Matching subtest and the NEPSY-II: Arrows and Block Construction tasks, if other measures are needed. Other tests of spatial reasoning are also available.

By *fluid reasoning* we mean the ability to engage with new information and exercise novel problem solving, and this could be executed via either verbal or nonverbal routes. On the WISC-IV this is represented by the fluid reasoning aspect of the PRI, albeit only nonverbal fluid as just mentioned, and again, these areas are also found on other measures. The WISC-IV manual (Wechsler, 2003) also suggests that Similarities and Word Reasoning can be considered measures of verbal fluid reasoning. Fluid reasoning, or novel problem solving, with its correlations with executive functioning (Hale & Fiorello, 2004), is likely to be a relative weakness for our students with NVLD, but may not be depending on how it

Table 8.3 Davis–Broitman assessment battery

| IQ | Executive functioning and attention | Memory | | Vis/verb integration | Sensory motor | |
		Visual	Verbal		Bilateral efficiency	Proprioceptive
WISC-IV, DAS-II, KABC-II, Stanford–Binet-V	CPT-II NEPSY-II: Attention and Response Set D-KEFS Subtests BRIEF	WRAML-II: Design Memory and Finger Windows tasks RCFT WISC-IV: Integrated Spatial Span task NEPSY-II: Memory for Designs task	WISC-IV: WMI tasks WRAML-II: Story Memory and Number Letter tasks CVLT WRAML-II: Verbal Learning subtest, NEPSY-II: List Learning task	NEPSY-II: Memory for Names WRAML-I or II: Sound Symbol Learning tasks	WRAVMA: Pegboard, NEPSY-II: Finger Tapping Other pegboard tasks	Observe pencil grip Observe amount of stress coming through on writing production

| Graphomotor | | Language | | Visual processing | Affect and behavior |
Timed	Untimed	Receptive	Expressive		
WISC-IV: PSI NEPSY-II: Visuomotor Precision PAL-II: Alphabet Writing	Beery-VMI-5 NEPSY-II: Design Copy WRAVMA: Drawing	WISC-IV: Integrated-Similarities, Vocabulary, and Comprehension PPVT-IV	WISC-IV: VCI TLC CASL EVT-III	WISC-IV: Symbol Search VMI-Visual NEPSY-II: Arrows task PAL-II Receptive and Expressive Coding Word Choice TOC	BASC-2 CRS-2 Achenbach series

| Academic testing | | |
Math	Reading	Writing
Wechsler Individual Achievement Test-III (WIAT-III) Key Math Test	WIAT-III Gray Oral Reading Test Nelson–Denny Reading Test Test of Word Reading Efficiency	WIAT-III The Oral and Written Language Test Test of Written Language-II

is operationalized. In Semrud-Clikeman, Walkowiak, Wilkinson, and Christopher's study (2010), deficits were found in fluid reasoning relative to both the AS and ADHD groups. But it is always the structure of the task, rather than what the task is called that will impact the students. For instance, the Stanford–Binet-V, has both a Nonverbal Fluid Reasoning and a Verbal Fluid Reasoning index score.

Although no studies of NVLD students were found utilizing this test, the two index scores clearly place very different spatial and language demands on a student (Roid, 2003). The Woodcock–Johnson-III: Test of Cognitive Abilities (Woodcock, McGrew, & Mather, 2001) would be another source of measures for fluid reasoning.

And finally, by *quantitative reasoning* we mean the ability to reason mathematically, utilizing number sense, quantities, etc. We have typically utilized the WISC-IV: Arithmetic and the Differential Ability Scales, 2nd edition (DAS-II): Sequential and Quantitative Reasoning (2007) tasks to measure this, but another interesting set of subtests can be found on the Stanford–Binet-V (Roid, 2003), the verbal and nonverbal quantitative reasoning measures. Berninger and Richards (2002) built quantitative reasoning into the underpinnings of their model for the development of math skills, and given the child with NVLD's propensity to develop math issues, this would be an important area to consider in an assessment.

Attention and Executive Functioning

By attention and executive functioning, we mean the ability to selectively focus and sustain attention to perform self-monitoring, organization, and planning required to accomplish a task. Whether there are differences between visual and verbal processes of attention and executive functioning has not been clearly established. However, Hain (2008) found that her group of students with NVLD had elevated scores on the Attention Problem and Learning Problem subscales on the Behavior Assessment System for Children–Teacher Report Form (BASC–TRF: Reynolds & Kamphaus, 2004) relative to her non-LD control group. Although this measure is not sensitive to specific cognitive functions per se, it is a valid ecological measure for attention and learning in a classroom environment. There are a few studies on nonverbal working memory, generally considered a type of executive function, which is hypothesized to be a relative weakness for children with NVLD and other children who are visuospatial processing disordered (Buchanann, Pavlocic, & Rovet, 1998; Cornoldi, Dalla-Vecchia, & Tressoldi, 1995; Liddell & Rasmussen, 2005). In addition Cornoldi, Rigoni, Tressoldi, and Vio (1999) found that "children with NVLD have difficulties with both the visual and the spatial components of visual working memory. However, their deficit with spatial components seems to be more severe [than the less spatial components]" (p. 55). There are newer speculations that some of the children with NVLD difficulties with social situations may also be due to executive functioning issues (Forrest, 2007); thus, assessment in this area may be especially important to consider.

To test for executive functioning, we believe that both cognitive tasks and rating scales should be used to understand how the child is functioning in this domain. We utilize the Conners Continuous Performance Test-II (CPT-II: Conners, 2000) for one measure of attention. Other possibilities are the Test of Variables of Attention (TOVA: Greenberg & Kindschi, 1996) or the Test of Everyday Attention for Children (TEA-Ch: Manly, Robertson, Anderson, & Nimmo-Smith, 2001) measures. Although none of these have been used in any research involving NVLD populations, we suggest that a computerized task with times exceeding at least 10-min duration would be important to uncover deficits in this population. We also use the NEPSY-II: Attention and Response Set subtests (Korkman, Kirk, & Kemp, 2007), although these are much shorter, as a verbal counterpoint to the CPT-II. The other attention/executive function subtests from the NEPSY-II can also be utilized, as well as select subtests of the Delis–Kaplan Executive Function System (D-KEFS: Delis, Kaplan, & Kramer, 2001). In terms of the rating scales, we use the Behavior Rating Inventory of Executive Function (BRIEF: Gioia, Isquith, Guy, & Kentworthy, 2000) which we find very helpful not only in understanding the child, but also in reinterpreting some of the child's behaviors to his/her parent and teacher as executive function issues rather than noncompliance, laziness, etc. All the information is useful in planning for interventions and accommodations/scaffolding for the student.

Learning and Memory

Learning and memory are those areas of cognitive functioning that enable us to encode new information, store it, and retrieve it when needed. Memory research on children with NVLD has been mixed. Liddell and Rasmussen (2005) found specific deficits on the Children's Memory Scale: Memory for Faces task (CMS: Cohen, 1997), while Silver, Ring, Pennett, and Black (2007), although not exactly studying the same populations, found no difference between visual short-term memory for those with isolated arithmetic deficits compared to those with reading and arithmetic deficits. Fine and Semrud-Clikeman (2010) theorize that children with NVLD should generally have better verbal memory than visual memory, especially on those tasks that tend to be more abstract and geometric. Our clinical work supports Fine and Semrud-Clikeman's position in that we tend to find NVLD students struggling more with the visual memory tasks, especially those that are more spatial and abstract and are less readily verbally encoded stimuli.

Similarly, we suggest that in measuring learning and memory it is important to consider whether the tasks are more visual, verbal, or visual/verbal integration tasks. We also suggest that these three important areas can be further broken down into information processing areas which can help us better understand the child's functioning and if other tests may be needed to clarify the situation. For each task, consider whether it evaluates immediate, working, or long-term memory. Does the task present real world objects or abstract geometric designs? Is it a strictly visual task, or one that can be easily mediated by language? Some tasks may be more contextualized (more semantic cues) and others more decontextualized (reduced semantic cueing). Another aspect to consider is how cognitively demanding the task is. Is it simple recognition and retrieval, or does it require higher level synthesis or sequential processing?

The verbal memory tasks in our battery usually include WISC-IV: WMI tasks, the WRAML-II: Story Memory (contextualized memory) and Number Letter (decontextualized memory) tasks (Sheslow & Adams, 2003), and then either the California Verbal Learning Test – Child Version (CVLT: Delis, Kaplan, Kramer, & Ober, 1994), the WRAML-II: Verbal Learning subtest, or the NEPSY-II: List Learning task. These memory/learning tasks tap into immediate memory with some semantic aspects without sequencing demands plus learning over time, dependent at least in part on executive functioning. Given the patterns we find among these results, we may use some other tasks as well. For our visual tasks, we tend to use the WRAML-II: Design Memory (abstract and spatial) and Finger Windows (spatial and sequential) tasks, the Rey Complex Figure Test and Recognition Trial (RCFT: Meyers & Meyers, 1995 – trying to capture a visual task with high executive function demands which also includes and immediate, delay and recognition tasks), the WISC-IV: Integrated Spatial Span task, and/or the NEPSY-II: Memory for Designs task. For the visual/verbal integration tasks we use the NEPSY-II: Memory for Names or the WRAML-I or II: Sound Symbol Learning tasks. Again, other acceptable measures are available.

Sensory Motor/Graphomotor

Here we are primarily referring to those processes that allow us to receive and send information from the sensory areas of the body to the brain and back again, with graphomotor being specific to proprioceptive feedback loops. Sensory motor/graphomotor issues have been considered a core deficit of NVLD since Rourke's early work (Harnadek & Rourke, 1994; Rourke, 1989; Rourke & Strang, 1978). In particular Rourke speaks of tactile perceptual deficits more pronounced on the left side of the body and bilateral psychomotor coordination deficiencies, again more on the left side of the body. Somewhat in support of this, Durand et al. (2005) found that her "results are consistent with previous findings that children with NLD show poor performance on pegboard tasks, although there is no evidence of general poor fine motor skills, in children with discrepancy-defined NLD" (p. 90). More recently, Wilkinson and Semrud-Clikeman (2008) did not find statistically significant differences among NVLD, ADHD: I, and control children on either the more simple (Finger Oscillation Test: also called the Finger Tapping Test: Spreen & Strauss, 1998) or more complex (Grooved Pegboard Test: Klove, 1963) motor speed measures, leading them to suggest that their data do not support at least that aspect of Rourke's model. In a study looking at finger tapping and visual processing efficiency, both nongraphomotor tasks, Landau, Auerback, Gross-Tur, and Shalev (2003) found that NVLD children were significantly slower than both their ADHD and control groups. Even when speeded performance, was not part of how the subjects were selected.

Although controversy continues regarding the role of sensorimotor functioning in NVLD populations, we do believe that these areas should be measured, as processing speed efficiencies are important to know about when considering various accommodations. We most often use the Wide Range Assessment of Visual Motor Abilities (WRAVMA: Adams & Sheslow, 1995) subtests, the Beery/VMI-5, the NEPSY-II: Design Copying, Finger Tapping and Visuomotor Precision tasks, and the WISC-IV: PSI tasks. Although we have not included it in our battery, the Dean–Woodcock Neuropsychological Battery (2003) has received good reviews and would seem to offer some useful subtests. Other aspects of processing that should be taken into account are grapho-symbol (WISC-IV: Coding) vs. grapho-nonsymbol (NEPSY-II: Visuomotor Precision) and timed vs. untimed. We also often use our Occupational Therapy colleagues to help collect data and plan interventions.

Language

This area has always been somewhat problematic for the field as the disorder is known as a Nonverbal Learning Disorder. Some originally mistook this as meaning that a child with this disorder had no language. This idea, hopefully, is gone. Many persons with NVLD have multiple language strengths (Johnson & Myklebust, 1967; Rourke, 1989, Voeller, 1986), such as vocabulary development, rote verbal memory, long-term verbal memory, and phonological awareness, but weaknesses in language development are also apparent. If we utilize the Bloom's (1988) domains of language forms, used by many speech and language professionals, we would say that NVLD children tend to have strengths in the areas of phonology, morphology, and syntax, and difficulties with some aspects of semantics and difficulties with pragmatics (Volden, 2004).

Problems in the area of semantics seem to arise in later latency and adolescence rather than the primary years, mainly because the language processing demands of the earlier grades do not challenge the relative weaknesses of children with NVLD (Rourke & Tsatsanis, 1996). These difficulties are then believed to affect aspects of both oral comprehension and reading comprehension (Mamen, 2007). In both oral and reading comprehension, there is a difficulty or inability to appropriately process metaphor, analogy, and inferential language (Schiff, Bauminger, & Toledo, 2009; Worling, Humphries, & Tannock, 1999). Looking even more closely at narrative comprehension, Humphries, Cardy, Worling, and Peets (2004) found that NVLD children were poorer in comprehending inferences, but not facts.

Pragmatic language has long been a concern for NVLD students. Pragmatics is generally considered to be the social discourse aspect of language (Rourke, 1995). In the older nomenclature of speech and language pathology, this was referred to as semantic–pragmatic disorder (Volden, 2004) and was a target of intervention by these practitioners. Research utilizing the Test of Language Comprehension (Wiig & Secord, 1989) by Crovetti (1998) and Dorfman (2000) does support that this is an area of weakness in NVLD students and suggests that this test is one with some clinical usefulness. Klin and Volkmar (2003) have also suggested evaluating turn taking, sensitivity to the other while in dialogue, eye gaze, and other nonverbal aspects of pragmatic communication.

Other processing areas to be considered include receptive vs. expressive language, timed vs. untimed measures of language production, more semantic vs. less semantic language reasoning and production, and free, cued, and/or recognition retrieval of verbal information. Our battery includes the WISC-IV: Similarities and Vocabulary subtests for semantic reasoning (and their WISC-IV: Integrated counterparts for receptive/recognition samples of language), and the WISC-IV: Comprehension subtest, the Test of Language Comprehension (Wiig & Secord, 1989), the Comprehensive Assessment of Spoken Language (CASL: Carrow-Woodfolk, 1999) for the pragmatic aspects. We often utilize our speech and language colleagues to help collect, evaluate, and interpret these data. Finally, we also look at rapid naming with the Comprehensive Test of Phonological Processing (CTOPP: all four rapid naming subtests) and verbal retrieval efficiency with either the D-KEFS: Verbal Fluency or NEPSY-II: Word Generation tasks. These measures were selected because information processing efficiency should be thought of as multifaceted, not just the WISC-IV: PSI, and should include phonological accessing efficiency and verbal fluency. The CTOPP was selected because it does have four measures of phonological accessing, and Rosemary Tannock (Tannock, Martinussen, & Frijters, 2000) has found that at least the color-naming task is more sensitive to executive function issues than the digit and letter tasks. In our clinical work we have also observed this as well as with the object naming task. Obviously this will need more experimental verification but currently can still provide useful clinical data. The verbal fluency measures are also fluency/efficiency measures and can also be used for their demands on executive functioning as well as examples of the contrast available between the more semantic retrieval (word) vs. nonsemantic retrieval (letter) which all add to our understanding of the strengths and weaknesses of the language system in children with NVLD.

Visual Processing

Visual processing consists of many things and is really more akin to the box that needs to be checked on an IEP than a specific measure. It tends to be the catch-all term that overlaps cognition, memory, and sensorimotor functions where vision is a significant part of the processing being done. Again, one of the most solid aspects of Rourke's (1989, 1995) theory of NVLD has to do with difficulties with visual-spatial processing in persons with NVLD. His primary finding in this arena was difficulties on the Judgment of Line Orientation test (JLO; Benton, Sivan, Hamsher, Varney, & Spreen, 1983). However, it is often hard to parse visual out from spatial and to control for whether any particular client may be verbally encoding and processing the material. Hain's (2008) finding (noted above) about the Symbol Search differences would support the notion of visual processing. However, the task also places demands on abstract design processing, much like the Block Design task, not more simple visual processing efficiency so this complicates the possible interpretations.

As suggested in the *Intellectual Assessment* and *Learning and Memory* sections, if we consider visuospatial reasoning and memory as a *visual processing* problem, in addition to a reasoning and memory difficulty, then again the data supporting difficulties in this area are strong and repeated over the many studies cited above. Other tasks we use to assess this area would be the NEPSY-II: Arrows task and measures of orthographic processing (especially at younger years) with the Process Assessment of the Learner-II: Receptive and Expressive Coding and Word Choice (PAL-II, 2007) and the Test of Orthographic Competence (Mather, Roberts, Hammill, & Allen, 2008).

Affect and Behavior

As reviewed in Chapter 3, socioemotional issues have long been considered an issue for NVLD children and adults (Bigler, 1989; Casey & Rourke, 1991; Little, 1993; Weintraub & Mesulam, 1983). However, how to measure these issues has not always been clear. Historically, Porter & Rourke (1985) used the Personality Inventory for Children (PIC; Wirt, Lachar, Klinedinst, & Seat, 1977). The PIC is a broad-based behavior rating scale that measures the parents' view of how their child is functioning. The newer version now has compatible self-report and teacher-report scales but tends to take longer to administer than the more popular Behavioral Assessment System for Children-2 (Reynolds & Kamphaus, 2004), Conners' Rating Scales-2 (2008), and the Achenbach (2001a, 2001b)) series of rating scales. We suggest that in evaluations for NVLD the clinician should start with broad-based behavior rating scales and then follow up with narrower band instruments in areas of concern to shorten evaluations performed as follow-ups to interventions.

Our position on projective techniques is that they can be a risky venture for students with NVLD. Given the verbosity and spatial issues, tests like the Rorschach could produce results making the person with NVLD look much more disturbed than they are. Apperception techniques, like the Robert's-2 (2001), appear to have more face validity, but there is no research on using them with an NVLD population, so results should be treated with great caution. Still, some of the cards with child-to-child interpersonal situations could provide quite valuable clinical information.

Aspects of the Vineland-2 (Sparrow, Cicchetti, & Balla, 2004) and the ABAS-II (Harrison & Oakland, 2003), especially the socialization and communication domains, can also be quite valuable in evaluating the day-to-day functioning of children with NVLD compared to their same-age peers. As with the other behavior rating scales Parent and Teacher forms are available and both of these adhere to the guidelines developed by the American Association of Intellectual and Developmental Disabilities.

Academic Assessment

Although academic assessment is often performed by the resource specialist or the educational therapist, the academic part of an evaluation should always be thought through with the team. We have found it useful to use standardized assessment measures in the academic part of the assessment. Clinically speaking, we prefer to have the academic testing done first so that we can better plan out who else will be involved in the team, and even at times what other tests should be included in the overall evaluation. Obviously all the basic academics must be covered to insure that the child's eligibility for IDEA-2004 is explored. For this we prefer the Wechsler Individual Achievement Test-III (WIAT-III, 2009) rather than the Woodcock–Johnson Achievement Battery-III. This is because in our experience the WIAT-III tends to better capture the clinical issues students with NVLD experience. However, since there is no specific research on this, it is open to a healthy debate. But we also believe that neither battery is quite sufficient. To our WIAT-III we add the Gray Oral Reading Test-IV (Weiderholt & Bryant, 2001), or for high-school or college level, the Nelson–Denny Reading Test (Brown, Fischo, & Hanna, 1993). We have also used the Test of Word Reading Efficiency (Torgesen, Wagner, & Rashotte, 1999), the Test of Written Language-4 (Hammill & Larsen, 2009), the Key Math- 3: Diagnostic Assessment (Connolly, 2007), and the Oral and Written Language Scales (Carrow-Woodfolk, 1995), depending on what the child's academic issues are.

Once an evaluation is complete, the real work begins: treatment. If an evaluation is thorough and thoughtful, it will provide important information that can guide interventions for mitigating and remediating NVLD symptoms.

Summary

In this chapter we discussed the need for and possible ways to screen for NVLD. In addition we have stressed the importance of a comprehensive evaluation and presented our model. Our model includes the eight general areas which we believe need to be considered. They are *IQ, Attention and Executive Functioning, Learning and Memory, Sensory Motor/Graphomotor, Visual Processing, Language, Affect and Behavior,* and *Academic Testing.* We also offer an information processing framework from which to begin to think about how to understand the test data. In addition we offer some examples of current tests which could be used to accomplish these goals in the assessment process. With a clear picture of the strengths and deficits for your child in hand the next step is creating a treatment plan. Chapter (9) offers general guiding principles regarding creating a comprehensive plan for treating children with NVLD.

Chapter 9
Treatment

"Treat early and often" is the refrain commonly heard, as most professionals believe that children with NVLD can and will learn, but it will take repeated, continual, and specific interventions (Tsatsanis & Rourke, 2003). Evidence suggests that the earlier and more accurate the diagnosis, coupled with early intervention, the better the outcome (Martin, 2007; Thompson, 1997). This chapter offers general guiding principles regarding treating children with NVLD. In Chapter 10, we will apply those principles to both schools and home.

The Need for Treatment

NVLD children are at high risk for a multitude of clinical concerns including depression, anxiety disorders, and social and academic issues (Rourke, 1988; Semrud-Clikeman, Walkowiak, Wilkinson, & Christopher, 2010). Since approximately 65% of meaning is communicated by nonverbal cues, such as tone of voice, facial expression, posture, and body language, there is potential for a significant difficulty in pragmatic communications for the child who cannot decipher or interpret nonverbal behavior (Nowicki & Duke, 1992; Thompson, 1997). Rourke (1988) argues that untreated, the NVLD profile represents a sufficient condition for the development of psychopathology. He notes that these children are at risk specifically for the development of what he called "internalizing" psychopathology (i.e., depression and anxiety). Rourke (1988) believes that this occurs because the child's nonverbal deficiencies (poor visual spatial, tactile-perceptual, psychomotor, and concept formation skills) and the child's overreliance on verbal skills (resulting in a parroting, repetitive style of speech) interfere with the development of social competency. He believes that this reduced social competency leads to isolation, low self-esteem, and the onset of depression and anxiety. In a recent study by Semrud-Clikeman et al. (2010) children with NVLD showed significant signs of sadness and social withdrawal compared to children with Attention Deficit Hyperactivity Disorder-Combined (ADHD-C), Attention Deficit Hyperactivity Disorder-Predominately Inattentive (ADHD-PI), and controls. Previous studies

J.M. Davis and J. Broitman, *Nonverbal Learning Disabilities in Children:*
Bridging the Gap Between Science and Practice, DOI 10.1007/978-1-4419-8213-1_9,
© Springer Science+Business Media, LLC 2011

have indicated that children with NVLD show signs of sadness particularly when they become older (Ozonoff & Rogers, 2003; Rourke, 2000).

Peck (1985) states that it is clear that youngsters with LD may suffer from loss of self-esteem, and in those cases where the children experience both pressure from the parents to succeed without additional support and stigmatization from their peers regarding their disability, their feelings of frustration and hurt may be so great as to place the young children at greater risk for later suicidal behavior. We suggest that these negative outcomes may be more common for children with NVLD than for neurotypical children. Earlier research (Rourke, Young, & Leenaars, 1989) suggested that individuals with an NVLD profile are at higher risk for suicide than any other learning disability subtype. However, more recent research (Semrud-Clikeman & Fine, 2010) has not supported this but has supported that the adolescent with NVLD has a higher incidence of sadness and social withdrawal than typically developing children. As the adolescent with NVLD feels more isolated, the propensity s/he has for serious depression and withdrawal increases. It would seem that increases in psychopathology are present along with reduced self-esteem and problems with emotional withdrawal. However, it is also true that some adolescents with NVLD can also become oppositional and many become vulnerable to victimization or manipulation (Semrud-Clikeman & Fine, 2010).

Not all agree with the above characterization. Kowalchuk and King's (1989) position is that empirical research has not yet demonstrated any causal link between the low self-esteem of a person with NVLD and increased suicide risk. Regardless of one's position on the database for suicidality, most express considerable concern regarding potential for developing future problems and agreement (Peck, 1985; Rourke et al., 1986; Semrud-Clikeman & Fine, 2010) on the need for early intervention.

What and when to treat is a complex clinical decision. The primacy of issues varies with the child's developmental level, as well as the individual strengths and deficits of the child with whom one is working. The family's means and resources must also be considered. As the potential areas of need cross over into many disciplines, a variety of professionals are likely to be involved in what would strongly believe have to evolve into a collaborative team model. A team coordinator or case manager would need to be established whose job it will be to keep all parties informed regarding the coordination of intervention services as well as the child's progress. A school psychologist would be in a good position to take this role; however, anyone might be so designated, including a parent. Thus, we are emphasizing that the successful treatment of a child with NVLD requires an interactive coordinated team. Let us begin with a review of some general organizing principles that could be of help guiding the team toward a successful collaboration.

General Intervention Guidelines

One of the most important concepts is to help the child and family understand that the child is not the disability. Children with NVLD, like all children, have strengths and weaknesses. It is crucial to help the child learn to understand and best use his/her unique mind. Many have supported this notion calling it islands of competencies (Brooks, 2001), multiple intelligences (Gardner, 1999), and the eight learning systems (Levine, 2002). The general rule is that the practitioner must teach the child what his or her strengths are and how he or she can best deal with the issue at hand. Whatever areas of strength emerge should be used as a vehicle for helping the child develop and maintain a strong sense of self-competency. In order to help keep these children motivated, we have to incorporate the child's passions into the treatment intervention plan.

Whoever is involved with the child must focus on achieving the following: clarifying language concepts, developing verbal reasoning, increasing comprehension and written output, improving social cognition, developing a sense of personal effectiveness, and protection from cognitive overload (Ahearn, 2010). Interventions should be direct and explicit, and they must involve the child and consist largely of verbal communication and modeling (Foss, 1991; Rourke, 1995). We will present models of or guidelines for intervention from several expert practitioners from a variety of disciplines who work with children with NVLD including Palombo, Little, Matte and Bolaski, Foss, and Tsatsanis and Rourke. The reader will see that there is considerable overlap and agreement across disciplines.

Palombo: A Clinical Social Worker's Perspective

Palombo (2006), a clinical social worker on the staff of the Rush Neurobehavioral Center in Chicago, views children with NVLD from a self-psychological perspective (for more information see Kohut, (1971)). He suggests that professionals should focus on interventions that increase the child's coping capacities and improve self-esteem. He believes that children with NVLD face many difficulties, including being socially disconnected and awkward, and are often teased and rejected. He believes this is primarily due to a lack of social competencies. He has observed that children with NVLD struggle to initiate conversation, tend to follow conventional scripts, have difficulty establishing empathy with peers, matching other's social skills, conceptualizing alternative scenarios, and using cause and effect reasoning, and they struggle with decoding social behavior. He believes that this is due in part to a mindblindness (Barron-Cohen, 1997); or a "theory of mind" problem with attributing mental states to oneself and others resulting in a difficulty making sense and predicting the behavior of others. He further suggests that these problems may be due to both receptive and expressive pragmatic language issues and executive function deficits. Palombo (2006) recommends that the child be explicitly taught about nonverbal communications including facial expressions, gaze, body posture, vocal intonation, tactile communication, and proximity. He also recommends that the clinician prepare the child for new situations by offering rehearsals or role plays, encouraging integration of all aspects of stories. He views social cognitive impairments as a significant area of deficit for NVLD children and recommends that they be taught social skills and strategies for understanding nonverbal communication in conjunction with mindsharing skills. By this he means that the child needs to be helped to speculate regarding why people take specific actions. The clinician must try to discuss empathy with the child, to teach social functioning, and to encourage the development of a sense of humor. He suggests that these things can be accomplished by having the clinician identify behaviors verbally, model behaviors to be learned, rehearse/practice potential actions/reactions with the child, and teach verbal mediation strategies. It will also be important to discuss and deal with feelings and to help the child to identify (decode) and express appropriate emotions. Palombo (2006) wants to help the child learn to mediate emotional states, in part by debriefing him or her following activities to help manage the anxiety in the moment. He also notes that medications can at times help with this.

Liza Little: Researcher and Medical Practitioner

Liza Little (1993) believes that interventions should reflect an ecological approach to the biopsychosocial needs of the child with NVLD. Like others, she notes that children with NVLD will need an interdisciplinary team of specialists. Children with NVLD need proper diagnosis, and typically a child neuropsychologist or school psychologist can provide this service. In addition, these children often need assessment by a developmental pediatrician or child psychiatrist for medication evaluation to help parents decide if medications may help some of the behavioral or psychiatric difficulties, referred to above, that are often comorbid with NVLD. Many children with NVLD are treated with stimulants for attentional issues, and moderate improvement from medication has been documented (Gross-Tsur, Ruth, Manor, & Amir, 1995; Rourke, 1995; Voeller, 1995). Antidepressants have also been used for anxiety and depression and there is some clinical documentation of trials with mood stabilizers as well (Ternes, Woody, & Livingston, 1987). Little further suggests that children with NVLD need individualized educational plans if they are in the public schools, or treatment plans if not, that take into account the nature of their deficits and strengths. This will include modifications, accommodations, and strategies to teach them the skills they need to develop (Thompson, 1997). A primary aid to the child's learning is to teach him or her sequentially and to use the child's verbal strengths to compensate whenever possible. The child will need training in social skills and pragmatics; these skills are not part of a curriculum or typical education plan. This is often done in groups, and finding these types of groups may be difficult, but as understanding of NVLD increases, so do the resources. These groups can be led by private clinicians or school psychologists, counselors, or speech and language therapists.

Matte and Bolaski and Foss: Educators

Matte and Bolaski (1998), both at Landmark College, note that in developing personal competence, assistance is needed for students with NVLD to learn and develop skills that reveal their personality and focus on and play to their strengths. Matte and Bolaski (1998) remind us that many students with NVLD tend to interpret language literally, which often leads to confusion for them and those around them. Furthermore, they tend to be limited in the skills of engaging in meaningful self-expression, seeing other points of view, and integrating life experience. One of their teaching examples is of a child with NVLD who is hitting the keys on a piano and an annoyed adult asks rhetorically, "Can you bang the keys a little harder?" The child responded with even more enthusiasm. Foss (1991) concurs, believing that clarifying language concepts should be a priority for these children. She further suggests that students with NVLD should be taught how to better understand part/whole relationships, to be able to compare and contrast relationships, and to better understand cause-and-effect and temporal/spatial relationships. Instruction in the meaning of verbal analogies and the promotion of self-questioning and self-monitoring strategies may also be useful. In addition, role modeling and role plays that focus on appropriate verbal responses and correct body language have the potential to improve interpersonal skills.

Many students with NVLD express a lot of empty, meaningless verbiage disconnected from an ongoing conversation and need help clarifying language concepts (Foss, 1991). To remediate this, students need strategies and to be supported in finding words that relate to and trigger understanding. She also notes that students with NVLD are often both unaware of their own and derive little or no meaning from vocal tone and pitch, facial expressions, gestures, and social conventions regarding touch and distance.

In addition, children with NVLD often need assistance with reading comprehension. Active reading strategies such as prereading, chunking, paraphrasing, and self-quizzing can be effective for improving comprehension. It may also be beneficial to have the child read out loud, concurrently with other active reading strategies. For example, orally prereading a textbook chapter or orally processing a visual aid in a textbook may trigger and/or increase understanding. Instructional efforts that help generate clear meanings can improve comprehension. A step-by-step, parts-to-whole teaching approach may help broaden perspective and increase recognition. This is because students with NVLD may focus only on small parts of an assignment while neglecting the larger picture (Foss, 1991). These small segments may be the baseline of comprehension, and, due to problem-solving deficits, it becomes necessary for the teacher to break down their lessons into micro-units. It is essential that assumptions regarding ability not be made, and that this step-by-step approach start where the student's skills begin to break down.

Foss (1991) has further suggested that improving social cognition consists of clear and concise instruction, practice in a controlled environment, encouragement, and constructive feedback. Because students with NVLD characteristics have difficulty with nonverbal communication, direct instruction should involve videotaping their role plays which can then be later analyzed by the student and the teacher. It is recommended that, whenever possible, remediation efforts involve a one-to-one, tutorial-type setting, as this individualized attention enhances the internalization of learned material.

Foss (1991) has observed that many individuals with NVLD have learned how to compensate for their disability by verbally persuading others (teachers, parents, counselors, siblings, etc.) to intervene for them when tasks or situations become too difficult. Matte and Bolaski (1998) warn that complying with such requests is a disservice and promotes incompetence. However, the practitioner must monitor and balance and/or titrate the level of frustration being experienced by the child so that the he or she is encouraged to increase his or her social skills repertoire but without becoming hopeless and disaffected. It is a therapeutic balancing act. Matte and Bolaski's (1998) say that in their clinical experience they have also found that honesty, clarity, and directness are essential in the child developing self-worth and self-awareness and in fostering an understanding and acceptance of ability rather than fostering overemphasis of disability. Rourke (1995) has stressed that it is necessary to cultivate realistic expectations for the person with NVLD, taking account of both assets and deficits. These authors concur and we suggest creating scaffolding from which the child can begin to develop skills. We believe that the key is *working with* children to help them increase their capacity for independent activity. Clinical experience suggests that children with NVLD have a strong desire and motivation to become more independent and successful. Whitney (2002) also suggests that clinicians need to bridge the gaps for their NVLD clients until they can develop the needed skills for themselves. We believe that these collaborations will develop competence and self-esteem.

Tsatsanis and Rourke: Seminal Researchers

Tsatsanis and Rourke (2003) beautifully summarize what they view as their most important guidelines for conceptualizing an intervention plan. They begin by emphasizing the need to utilize the child's strengths to remediate the areas of weakness. A thorough evaluation is crucial, followed by creating a well-educated and coordinated team of professionals. What follows is a summary of Rourke's (1995) original 15-point approach to treatment (amended by Tsatsanis & Rourke, 2003):

1. *Observe the child's behavior closely; especially in novel or complex situations.* Here Rourke is cautioning the profession to focus on what the child does rather than what he or she might say. He believes that the child's actual behavior should be our guide to understanding his or her struggles. It is generally understood that the new or novel situations will most likely generate the greatest problems for the child with NVLD. Directly observing the child will allow the professional to develop an intervention plan that focuses more specifically on the needed skills.

2. *Adopt realistic attitudes.* The professional must use his or her refined under-standing of the child's strengths and weakness to plan for success. If there is no way for a school to accommodate the child's deficits, alternative programs must be found. In cases where this is not possible the family should be helped to avoid the situation.

3. *Teach the child in a systematic "step-by-step" fashion.* Rourke cautions that it is easy to misjudge the child's capacity to take in information. The child's supe-rior verbal skill often leads professionals to overestimate the NVLD child's overall skills and abilities. They note that instruction needs to be broken down and expressed verbally in simple sequential rules that children can follow even though they have these verbal abilities.

4. *Encourage the child to describe in detail important events that are transpiring in his or her life.* Rourke recognizes that the child with NVLD often misunder-stands the significance of his or her behavior. He suggests that engaging in a detailed discussion of an event can allow the child to hear the discrepancies between his or her perception and the perception of others. Using a technique of reteaching can allow the professional to check what the child has analyzed and integrated.

5. *Teach the child appropriate strategies for dealing with particularly trouble-some situations that occur on a frequent everyday basis.* Rourke notes that generalization is difficult for children with NVLD and specific detailed step-by-step solutions will be helpful.

6. *Encourage generalizations of learned strategies and concepts.* Rourke reminds us that children with NVLD often have pervasive deficits in the judgment of cause and effect relationships. They will not make the inference that there is a relationship between their action and the resulting consequence. It is necessary for the professional to repeat the lesson in a step-by-step fashion, again and again, in a variety of settings.

7. *Teach the child to refine and use appropriately his or her verbal skills.* Rourke suggests that the child with NVLD needs to be taught *what to say, how to say it, and when to say it.* Considerable time should be spent training and retraining the child to stop, look, listen, and weigh alternatives even in the most mundane circumstances. Failure to do so leaves the child subject to negatively reinforc-ing consequences which can promote a withdrawal and avoidance.

8. *Teach the child to make better use of his or her visual–perceptual–organiza-tional skills.* Rourke observes the child's tendency to lead with his or her strong suit and attempt to avoid focusing on those skills which are more problematic. He cautions professionals to help the child to exercise and develop his or her less-developed skills to work toward achieving the highest level possible through age-appropriate remedial exercises.

9. *Teach the child to interpret visual information when there is competing audi-tory information.* Here Rourke is anticipating the complexity of new social situ-ations which are likely to be particularly challenging for the child with NVLD. He suggests that this be singled out for repeated instruction once an adequate basis has been previously reached.

10. *Teach appropriate nonverbal behavior.* Rourke suggests the professional teach the child with NVLD how specifically to do it. Reminding us that the child often does not know when to smile, when not to smile, when to move, where to look, etc. He recommends the use of a mirror or video equipment that can allow a detailed analysis of behavior.
11. *Facilitate structured peer interactions.* Here Rourke acknowledges the difficult tension between protecting vulnerable children with NVLD from failure while simultaneously trying to expand their horizons. He suggests the use of clubs and community groups, more structured social situations, as vehicles for promoting the careful development of successful peer interactions. Therapeutically oriented social skills groups are another valuable tool.
12. *Promote, encourage, and monitor systematic explorative activities.* While Rourke encourages the professional to engage the child with NVLD in social activities, he warns that it is imperative to offer sufficient verbal guidance and structure.
13. *Teach the child to use age-appropriate aids to reach a specific goal.* These may include digital watches, calculators, laptops, and various forms of assistive technologies which could be utilized to help improve the child's performance.
14. *Help the child develop insight into situations that are easy for him or her and those that are particularly troublesome.* Here Rourke is stressing the importance for the child [or adult] to understand his or her own cognitive functioning with the goal of developing a realistic understanding of his or her capacities. Once achieved, this understanding can help guide the child to get assistance when needed, and to help him or her avoid situations that may be more likely to end in failure.
15. *Be cognizant of the professional's role in preparing the child with NVLD for adult life.* Professionals have a unique and crucial role in helping the child plan for and achieve success. Lastly, Rourke differentiates our role from that of any other educators with a particular specific curriculum to cover. Our domain is as vast as all of life, since the child with NVLD needs help accruing all life's social and survival skills.

Summary

In this chapter we emphasize the need for a team coordinator to manage the complex communications needed among the multitude of practitioners involved in treating a child with NVLD. We presented guidelines for intervention from several expert practitioners from a variety of disciplines who work with children with NVLD including Palombo, Little, Matte and Bolaski, Foss, and Tsatsanis and Rourke. The reader will see that despite the fact that these clinicians represented different professions there is considerable overlap and agreement across disciplines. They agree with meeting the child where he or she is, scaffolding the intervention to plan for success, removing the scaffolding slowly when convinced that the child has internalized the lessons, and that verbal mediation is most likely the key strategy for helping the child encode the necessary lessons. We are all are in agreement that it is crucial to for success include planning for generalization and transfer of the skills from the clinician's office to the real worlds of home, school, playground, and community. In Chapter 10 we will apply these general principles to two settings, the school and the home.

Chapter 10
Applying Guidelines

In this chapter we will apply the general principles previously discussed to two settings, schools and in the home. We will present the views and suggestions of several clinicians who represent our perspective on best practices. In Chapter 11 we will identify interventions that are targeted to specifically identified symptom areas.

School Settings

Here we will review the suggestions of three noted clinicians: Tanguay, Molenaar-Klumper, and Martin, regarding how the professional can assist to maximize school success for the child with NVLD. We would also like to emphasize that the following authors are speaking about students with NVLD in general, not a specific child. No two children with NVLD are alike, and therefore various and differing settings are needed to meet the needs of each particular child. We present these suggestions individually in their own right because each clinician comes from a different discipline and we believe it is of interest to let each speak from that discipline's perspective.

Tanguay

Tanguay (2002), author, advocate, and founder of "NLD on the Web," notes that children with NVLD are often late developers and are frequently prone to anxiety. She cautions that there is a great need to help the family prepare for maximum school success. She suggests helping the child to develop anxiety management strategies. Consistent routines are helpful, and when possible, arrange for the child to meet teachers/tutors before school starts. Tanguay (2002) believes that children with NVLD will need particular help in interpreting social cues during unstructured periods such as lunch or recess. These students need help learning to conform to the social milieu and professionals must work to create safe places, both at home and at school, where the child can decompress. She further observes that these

J.M. Davis and J. Broitman, *Nonverbal Learning Disabilities in Children:*
Bridging the Gap Between Science and Practice, DOI 10.1007/978-1-4419-8213-1_10,
© Springer Science+Business Media, LLC 2011

children often find it difficult to open their lockers and change quickly for gym, for example, and strategies tailored to meet these needs should also be considered. She suggests that professionals pay attention to the potential impact of physical layout, lights and sounds, crowds, and schedules when helping a family choose and/or prepare for a school.

Tanguay also directs school-based personnel to pay attention to the school's consistency, structured predictable days, classroom size, and number of teachers and/or aides. Teacher substitutions should be infrequent and classes with shared teaching should be avoided, as continuity offers the best chance for success. She lists the following guidelines for maximizing school success:

– Keep behaviorally challenged children or children who are noisy or fidgety away from students with NVLD
– Circle time is not effective; student should sit near and facing teacher/front row, not close to others
– Less visual distraction on walls/boards
– Do not leave children with NVLD unsupervised – they are often the targets for teasing and bullying
– Make careful pick-up and drop-off arrangements

She lists the following educational recommendations because NVLD student's learning styles are concrete and literal they therefore need specific directions and accommodations such as:

– Rubrics (scoring criteria) can be very effective as they plot the direction that needs to be taken specifically guiding the learner to broader skill development in a very concrete specific fashion
– Outlines, and for some, graphic organizers can help organize written work because they are unimodal learners
– Do not require the student to listen and write at the same time
– Because of difficulty in visual tracking, reduce information on a page, and use flip chart to separate concepts when needed
– Preteach material and provide notes ahead of lectures in the upper grades; front-load expectations, remind of context, and review prior knowledge
– Formal cooperative learning can be successful – if care is taken in arranging groups; one teacher is best

Tanguay (2002) believes that both public and private schools can be options for the child with NVLD, depending on the accommodations allowed. The public school system may meet a child with NVLD's needs with additional support services; special education in school can be delivered via full inclusion, resource services, or special day classes depending on the individual needs of the child. Services can include speech and language intervention, occupational therapy, etc. She observes these interventions to be most successful in elementary school where there is generally more structure; however, she expresses more concerns as school structure changes. Middle schools may have too many changes and multiple teachers to easily create a safe structure for the child. Some charter schools might be an option.

She believes that many charter schools tend to have a simpler physical layout, smaller classes, less disruptive populations, and a higher continuity of students and staff. Some private schools may also work; however, they will not be an option for all children with NVLD due to financial constraints and their admission processes. Moreover, some private schools are not able to provide services and accommodations that would be sufficient for children with NVLD. Lastly, home schooling might also be considered.

Molenaar-Klumper

Molenaar-Klumper (2002), an orthopedic pediatrician, generally concurs with Tanguay in that it is crucial to set up a learning environment that will play to the child's strengths. She offers some additional recommendations such as arranging books and supplies such that there will be no need to go back and forth to get items, providing a map of school and guidance getting to specialists, and arranging a buddy system. Pre-teaching and reviewing instructional content is also suggested, with the warning to be cautious and make sure to test for generalization. As we stated in the last chapter, students with NVLD frequently struggle with the transfer and generalization of new skills to different contexts. Therefore, any plan for success must include thinking about how this generalization is to be accomplished and how to evaluate whether or not it has been successful. She suggests using no figurative speech, no irony, and making sure that instruction starts at the concrete level and moves slowly to the more abstract. She also recommends close attention to school setting and class size while acknowledging that there is no set answer as to what is the best circumstance for children with NVLD. Some emphasize small classes with high structure; however, the most important factor is the skill of the teachers. Social skills and pragmatic training is critical for these students.

Martin

Martin (2007), a learning specialist, stresses that finding a school that is open-minded, flexible, and willing to consider the unique needs of each child is critical. She encourages parents to find a school that will meet the needs of the *whole* child, not just the remediation; recognizing their strengths as well as their challenges. She offers the following key elements for her version of the *ideal* school:

- It would have a small building with a simple logical layout; if not possible, then the ability to limit the child's classes to one section of the school
- Any numbering systems such as for classrooms would need to be clear and logical
- Classes occur in one or few classrooms with few doors
- Limited number of places to find one's things (lockers, cubbies, desks, closets) near to each other

- Low stimulation environment with few distractions
- Limited numbers of teachers, preferable for long periods of time. Block schedules may be useful
- Small structured classes with a consistent schedule and preteach the locations of any room changes
- Willing to allow extra time for class changes
- Teaching staffs that are trained in understanding the need of children with NVLD willing to assist children with difficult academic subjects through verbal explanations
- A safe, tolerant, consistent environment that minimizes competition and has no tolerance for bullying
- Supervised, structured social experiences and willing to provide help deciphering rules
- Availability of speech therapy for semantic language
- Opportunities for children to participate in speech-rich activities such as theater and foreign languages

All three of the perspectives above stress the importance of creating a school environment that reduces the chances of sensory overstimulation and confusion. Evaluating the availability of services, including social skills training and alternative learning opportunities, appears to be important as well. In addition, it cannot be overstressed that planning must include both the interventions for the particular child and for the transfer and generalization of that learning to new contexts. Although children spend most of their waking day in school, the influence of the home environment should not be underestimated. Some researchers have given particular thought to the needs of parents of children with NVLD, and how best to manage life at home, as discussed below.

Working with the Families

Professionals will be called upon to work very closely with the parents of children with NVLD. It is imperative that an inclusive, collaborative, and respectful team relationship be developed. Little (1993), whose research program focuses on understanding the victimization experiences of children on the autism spectrum and the prevention of negative health outcomes for children with disabilities, explored the needs of mothers who have children with NVLD. The results from her 2003 study suggest that a majority of mothers perceived the education of teachers and their own education as central priorities.

The other domain of needs that mothers considered very important was in the realm of educational services for their children. In particular, social skills training for their child was perceived as one of their top three needs. Although there has been an increase in available information over the last 20 years on NVLD (Klin, Volkmar, & Sparrow, 2000a; Klin, Volkmar, Sparrow, Cicchetti, & Rourke, 2000b), it is notable that the majority of mothers in Little's study perceived knowledge deficits as major needs. Her findings suggest that some children with these disorders are not accessing necessary and vital services and hypothesize that this is because of problems with availability, a lack of education in teachers, and possible communication problems between families and school professionals. She fears that the parents of children with NVLD do not have easy, clear access to educational services and do not necessarily know what they are entitled to ask for or how to get these services from their schools in order to help their children.

Little's data further suggest that most schools, both public and private, are simply not providing critical services, such as pragmatics and social skills training, in a way that is effective for a significant number of children with NVLD. Her finding that larger numbers of older students with NVLD are leaving the public education system for private schools also suggests that educational needs, such as smaller class sizes, social skill interventions, and adequate vocational training, may be lacking for the adolescent (Little, 2003). Her data also suggest that school and mental health professionals, such as guidance counselors and mental health therapists, were perceived as some of the least helpful resources to children with NVLD and that it seems like they will need additional training to help them better understand these children and to provide better services for them.

Another finding (Little, 1999; Woodbury, 1993) is that the child with NVLD may well be the child who shows up in the school nurse's office a great deal with a variety of somatic symptoms. These symptoms may be related to their psychological discomfort. She believes that professionals must empower parents by educating them on the symptoms and neurological basis of NVLD. Pamphlets, checklists, web sites, and source books should be recommended. Parents need to be educated to advocate for their children's physical, academic, and social needs, and to demand that schools and health professionals recognize the problems of children with NVLD.

Little (1999), herself a nurse, notes that once a diagnosis is made several safety issues emerge of particular importance to a school nurse that should be discussed with parents. She believes that children with NVLD are particularly prone to getting hurt. Although nurses educate all parents about safety for their children, Little feels that children with NVLD are at greater risk than their typically developing peers. Small children therefore need uncluttered and less dangerous environments (Thompson, 1997). Little warns that these children should be supervised carefully on slides and Jungle-Gyms because of their poor coordination and visual-spatial problems. Crossing streets, biking, turning on hot water, and learning to use the stove are areas that need specific teaching. Instruction should be verbal, sequential, and repeated many times, because these children do not apply learning from one situation to another.

Little (1999) also suggests that risk for victimization is higher. Since children with NVLD do not effectively process nonverbal communication or social cues, they are easy targets for ridicule and exploitation by peers, adults, and parents. She encourages professionals to talk about each new social situation with the child and family. She recommends describing typical behavior and typical reactions. She believes that it is crucial to teach parents that becoming angry at these children is very easy, and recommends that it is vital to teach parental coping strategies to help with the frustration.

Finally, Little's (1999) findings indicate that children with NVLD are prone to be sedentary and to avoid physical activity that challenges their disabilities. She warns that as the child matures, weight may become a problem, in part due to the child's reluctance to be physically active. She recommends talking with parents about types of activities to promote physical health. For example, the child with NVLD may be able to learn how to shoot baskets if allowed to practice over and over again. However, being expected to know how to play effectively as part of a team in a game requires a different level of complexity and may prove exceptionally taxing.

Antshel & Guy-Ronald (2006) found that the greatest source of stress in their sample of mothers of children aged 8–11 who have NVLD was dysfunctional interactions with their child. Diminished social skills are often a prominent component of the profile of children with NVLD. Given these data, it may be beneficial to consider social skills training as a means of not only improving the child's peer relations but also positively affecting maternal stress levels. Given that (a) children with NVLD are often comorbid for ADHD and (b) parenting stress is also commonly reported in ADHD (e.g., Harrison & Sofronoff, 2002), it may also be beneficial to consider the role that parent behavioral management training interventions (see Barkley, 1997, for a sample program) may play in reducing maternal stress in NVLD. For example, in the ADHD literature, there is robust support for parenting training in behavioral management for reducing parenting stress (Pelham, Wheeler, & Chronis, 1998). Although there are very few data on the efficacy of parent training groups in children with NVLD, Antshel & Guy-Ronald (2006) speculate that this intervention may also be fruitful in children with NVLD.

Martin (2007), herself the mother of a child with NVLD, acknowledges the burden parents of children with NVLD have to create a safe home environment. She stresses the importance of providing a psychologically safe refuge free from the exhausting demands of the outside world. Just accomplishing the basic learning activities can be exhausting for these children. They will also have a greater need for parental assistance in all areas of life over the course of their lifespan. Parents will need assistance in managing these tasks without fears of infantilizing their children (Rourke, 1985) or making them overly dependent. Professionals can and must help parents recognize the appropriateness of parental intervention and involvement (Whitney, 2002). Professionals should teach parents to understand why their children are more vulnerable so they can advocate for their children. Armed with knowledge, parents can correct the ignorance which often fuels the criticisms leveled at them. Martin (2007) cautions that it takes a great deal of time to act as their mediator to the world but offers the following suggestions to make the time worthwhile:

• Ask them questions to stretch their thinking
• Help them to see patterns – to understand and anticipate routines and schedules

- Explicitly explain the use of schedules
- Develop an open and nonjudgmental relationship which will promote their allowing you to know what they need help with
- Regularly check in with them regarding how things are going
- Specifically ask about their social interactions and demystify the novelty
- Encourage their reflectivity through modeling finding solutions to challenges
- Make your home a "psychological" haven for the child
- Limit the number of new experiences so that they have the ability to practice and master tasks
- Accept that homework will take longer and your child will need your assistance and work with the school to best manage assignments for relevance
- Keep duplicates of books to avoid the issues related to forgetting to bring them home
- Allow them to dictate to you when constructing maps and graphs and diagrams
- Practice activities (such as taking the bus) so that they will be successfully able to manage on their own and obtain as much independence and autonomy as they can.

Martin (2007) addresses the need for families to step in and help their child progress in an appropriate developmental fashion, noting that each child will have different skills. Some may never learn to drive, while others can become good drivers with assistance. The life skills required for independent living such as managing a checkbook, laundry, cooking, and housekeeping will have to be carefully and explicitly taught. Martin goes on to reflect upon the difficulty families have balancing their wishes to promote their child's independence and the realities that require additional interventions. She encourages a progressive approach in which one withdraws support whenever it is no longer needed, but is ever ready to put them back in if the child encounters something new and novel and cannot quite figure out how to access and generalize previously learned material.

Summary

In this chapter we reviewed the suggestions of three noted clinicians: Tanguay, Molenaar-Klumper, and Martin, regarding how the professional can assist to maximize school success for the child with NVLD. All of them stress the importance of creating a school environment that reduces the chances of sensory overstimulation and confusion. Evaluating the availability of services, including social skills training and alternative learning opportunities, appears to be important as well. Also of import is the key role of collaboration. The team approach is required given the often many types of interventions students with NVLD require. In addition, we presented suggestions on how to assist families on how to create the most supportive environment for their child with NVLD. All practitioners note that the needs of the individual child must be taken into account and a case-specific flexible plan must be created to meet those needs, and again, in a collaborative, flexible, problem-solving fashion. In Chapter 11 we will offer examples of specific intervention aimed to target specific deficits for children with NVLD.

Chapter 11
Interventions

In this chapter we will identify specific, more focused interventions that have been suggested for children with NVLD utilizing the umbrella of principles for intervention discussed in Chapter 7. Unfortunately, as Matte and Bolaski (1998) note, intervention research on NVLD is very limited leaving us few empirically based options from which to choose. Little (2003) concurs, adding that there is also little consensus within the clinical or educational fields wherein the most critical needs and services need to be delivered to children with NVLD (see also Klin, Volkmar, & Sparrow, 2000a; Klin, Volkmar, Sparrow, Cicchetti, & Rourke, 2000b). In an era where the least restricted environment and/or full inclusion in large mainstream classrooms is often the intervention of choice for children with disabilities, Little suggests that it is of paramount importance that educational systems provide evidence of the efficacy of their services for children with less well-known disabilities and complex needs, such as children with NVLD. For a broader review and critique of full inclusion see Kauffman and Hallahan's *The Illusion of Full Inclusion – 2nd Edition* (2005).

Antshel & Guy-Ronald (2006) suggest that a "one size fits all" approach may not maximize outcomes; hypothesizing that within NVLD, child variables will be important to consider when designing interventions. For example, they found that the greatest source of stress in their sample of mothers of children who have NVLD was dysfunctional interaction with their child. Given this, they suggest that it may be beneficial to consider social skills training (SST) as a means of not only improving the child's peer relations but also positively affecting maternal stress levels and thus improving parent–child interactions. In addition, they state that the severity of a child's internalizing symptoms is a strong predictor of maternal stress for the mothers of children with NVLD, although they note that there is not a strong research base that has previously reported maternal stress in the pediatric depression literature. Though certainly requiring replication, they suggest that interventions addressing internalizing symptoms for children with NVLD may be beneficial for both the child and the child's mother. Hopefully, future studies will explore this possibility.

Individual specialists in related fields (occupational therapists, physical therapists, educational therapists, school psychologists, developmental pediatricians, etc.)

J.M. Davis and J. Broitman, *Nonverbal Learning Disabilities in Children:*
Bridging the Gap Between Science and Practice, DOI 10.1007/978-1-4419-8213-1_11,
© Springer Science+Business Media, LLC 2011

have developed clinical treatment guidelines for interventions that are thought to be helpful, but thus far little empirical research has evaluated the helpfulness or outcomes of these interventions or services (Atwood, 2007; Klin, Volkmar, & Sparrow, 2000a; Klin, Volkmar, Sparrow, Cicchetti, & Rourke, 2000b; Rourke, 1995; Schopler, Mesibov, & Kunce, 1998; Thompson, 1997). Unfortunately, we have found no literature on the effect of various variables, such as the child's age, gender, or the family's income and education, on differences in helpfulness of various resources. Treatment outcome studies that examine the efficacy of services for children with AS and NVLD are also rare. Semrud-Clikeman and Fine (2010) suggest that intervention for children with NVLD will need to encompass several aspects of daily life. Academic interventions are often needed to support children with mathematics, writing, and planning/organization. Social and emotional interventions can improve functioning at home and school, and support resiliency into adulthood. They also lament that there is no available research to support the efficacy of the most utilized interventions. Strategies have been developed through suggestions from clinical reports and common sense given the profile of strengths and deficits seen in children with NVLD. Attaining data on needs and the availability and helpfulness of resources tailored to those needs are critical to the process of developing standards of treatment for these children (Soriano, 1995).

Specific Interventions

We have found that the major categories of deficits and dysfunction for children with NVLD can be usefully separated into: *motor coordination, visual-spatial/ sensory perception, executive functioning, social/emotional deficits, intellectual reasoning*, and *academic programs*. We will offer a few sample interventions for each of these categories. Lastly, we will discuss the use of psychotherapy for children with NVLD. We remind the reader that few if any of these have an empirical basis and are offered for illustrative purposes only.

Motor Coordination

Children with NVLD may need the assistance of an occupational therapist that can help the child develop fine and/or gross motor control. Such children often have poor fine and gross motor coordination, severe balance problems, and difficulties with graphomotor skills. They were probably late learning to tie their shoes or ride a bike – or they may never have learned at all. They may have trouble catching a ball. They may write slowly, and their handwriting may be illegible (Davis & Broitman, 2006). For handwriting, some (e.g., Martin, 2007) have found that moving from printing to handwriting early helps alleviate writing challenges for children with NVLD, while others (Berninger & Richards, 2002) say that if a child is having trouble printing, moving to cursive can create two dysfluent systems and that printing efficiency should be the focus. Both sets of researchers seem to agree that when the physical act of writing is severely challenging, moving the child to a keyboard-based or voice-activated system is advised.

Interventions

1. Occupational therapy/physical therapy – teaching movement with words.
2. Loops and other groups: Kinesthetic Writing System (1999) by Mary Benbow emphasizes the motor skills needed to form letters.
3. The grotto grip (http://www.grottogrip.com) is a plastic grip that attaches to a pencil to help a student learn the correct way to hold the pencil.
4. Keyboarding Skills (1986) by Diana King helps the student learn the keyboard using verbal cues.
5. Games and activities that develop fine motor skills and visual perception such as juggling and drumming. May be borrowed through your local library through the National Lekotek Center, http://www.lekotek.org.
6. Handwriting Without Tears (http://www.hwtears.com) developed by Jan Olsen has been used with some success in the schools, by clinical report.
7. Helping Children Overcome Learning Difficulties (1979) by Jerome Rosner offers specific suggestions on improving motor skills.

Visual-Spatial/Sensory Perception

Children with NVLD often have a lack of image formation, poor visual recall, and faulty spatial perceptions. "They may get lost easily, or have difficulty finding things that are in plain sight. They may not be able to tell their left from their right." (Judy Lewis, NLDline).

Interventions

1. Optometric exercises – David Gresham's method (Griffin & Gresham 2002) to improve the eye tracking system.
2. Direct instruction through educational therapy/tutoring.
3. Photography classes – by learning how to capture visual images on paper child can develop better perception (Martin, 2007).
4. The Source for Visual-Spatial Disorders (2002) by Neff, Neff-Lippman, and Stockdale offers suggestions for help learning to drive (Martin, 2007).
5. Juggling (Draganski, Gaser, Busch, Schuierer, Bogdahn, & May, 2004) In the study, published in the Jan. 22 issue of *Nature*, researchers divided a group of young adults who had no experience in juggling into two groups. One group was

given 3 months to learn how to juggle three balls simultaneously, and the others remained nonjugglers. MRI scans were performed at the start of the study, after the jugglers became skilled performers and could juggle for at least 60 s, and 3 months later. During that 3-month period, the jugglers did not practice or attempt to extend their skills. Although the participants had similar brain scans at the start of the study, the second scan revealed that the jugglers experienced significant expansion in the area of the brain associated with the processing and storage of complex visual motion.

The amount of expansion also correlated with the juggler's performance. The more skilled they became, the greater growth they experienced. The increased areas seen on brain scans (among the jugglers) declined by the third brain scan. The nonjugglers showed no change in brain structure during the study.

Researchers say the temporary brain structure changes occurred in motion-selective areas of the brain, and the mechanism behind these changes is unclear and merits further study. Although this study was done with neurotypical participants, one author's anecdotal experience teaching juggling to children with NVLD suggests that it could be helpful (with a much longer training period involved).

Executive Functioning

Children with NVLD often have problems with organization which includes: decision making, planning, initiative, assigning priority, sequencing, motor control, emotional regulation, problem solving, planning, impulse control, establishing goals, monitoring results of action, self-correcting, working memory, and problems with spatial relations.

Interventions

1. Behavior Rating Inventory of Executive Function's™ (BRIEF®) Intervention Manual by Gerard A. Gioia, PhD, Peter K. Isquith, PhD, Steven C. Guy, PhD, Lauren Kenworthy, PhD. The BRIEF consists of three rating forms – a parent questionnaire, child self-report, and a teacher questionnaire – designed to assess executive functioning in the home and school environments and a manual. The manual offers behavior interventions geared to the results of the rating scales.
2. Skills for School Success (Archer and Gleason, Curriculum Associates Inc.; 4th Printing edition, January 1989).
3. Landmark Organizational Skills (Joan Sedita Landmark Study Skills Guide, Learning Disabilities: Information and Resources Landmark Foundation, September 1989).
4. The Kurzweil Study Skills Guide, and Teaching the Language Arts Tutorial Spectronics (2006), http://www.spectronicsinoz.com.

5. Individual tutoring with organization therapist (e.g., in Northern California: SOS skills for success – http://www.sos4students.com Beth Samuelson).
6. Software programs such as Inspiration®, Kidspiration® (Inspiration Software, 2008) and Don Johnston's Draft Builder (http://www.donjohnston.com) help students develop report ideas using webs, which are then converted into outline form.

Social/Emotional Deficits

Children with NVLD often have difficulties comprehending nonverbal communication, such as facial expression, body language, and tone of voice. They may not process efficiently and/or understand shrugs, winks, grins, or wrinkled foreheads. They may have trouble adjusting to transitions and novel situations, along with deficits in social judgment such as difficulty gauging appropriate personal space and social interaction (Thompson, 1997).

Traditional social skills training programs, captured by phrases like friendship groups or play groups, have not been found to be successful for children with NVLD without adjusting the intervention to address the types of perceptual and inferential thinking problems found with this diagnosis (Semrud-Clikeman & Schaefer, 2000). Semrud-Clikeman and Fine (2010) point out that one of the main issues with most social skills programs is that they begin at a level that does not directly train interpretation of facial expressions and body language. They feel that direct teaching of social perception skills through practice, modeling, and role-playing is likely most helpful. Teaching social perception through task analysis and rule teaching allows the child with NVLD to verbally process the information and use his/her strengths to learn new skills. They go on to say that the intervention needs to progress slowly with plenty of structure and time for the child to practice foundational skills before moving on to the more complex activities that require the building of trust to attempt them. For generalization of skills to occur, parent and teacher involvement are important to allow for practice of newly learned skills (Semrud-Clikeman & Fine, 2010).

Interventions

1. *Social Competence Intervention Program* (Guli et al., 2008) has been designed to work with children with NVLD and Asperger's Disorder. SCIP is an intervention that is multisensory in nature and targets underlying difficulties in social perception as well as providing exercises to improve the generating of strategies for problem solving. The SCIP exercises were adapted from children's creative drama and theater classes and provide practice in developing an accurate perception and response to facial and vocal cues. The exercises move

from perception of emotions to interpretation and then to response. Initially, the child sees pictures of faces and with mastery of emotional recognition and labeling is presented with naturalistic vignettes of children interacting. As the child progresses through the program, he/she is introduced to understanding his/her own emotions and then those of others. The work is constantly reviewed and supported throughout the time of the intervention thus providing for review and refreshing of skills. The activities that are part of SCIP are reported by the children to be fun.

Guli (2005) evaluated the efficacy of the SCIP program. In this study the children improved in their ability to correctly recognize facial expressions as well as vocal cues following the intervention. Qualitative results showed that 75% of parents reported one or more positive changes in social perception or competence after participating in the intervention, while 82% of the children reported one or more positive effects of the intervention. Thus, this study's results suggest that effects may generalize over settings (i.e., home and school). The results of this study lend support to efficacy of the SCIP program that targets specific difficulties in a very specialized population. Moreover, these findings strongly support research that stresses training in perception and integration of nonverbal cues for children with nonverbal learning disabilities (Barnhill, Tapscott, Tebbgenkamp, & Smith, 2002).

2. *Parent Effectiveness Training (PET)* and general programs for parental involvement (Gordan, 2006) have been used with children with NVLD. In addition to these manualized programs, parents are recommended to provide opportunities for their child to participate in organized activities such as Boy or Girls Scouts, 4-H, and other structured experiences. In cases where the family has social difficulties, family therapy has often been recommended (Carlson & Christenson, 2005). While some parents may not be temperamentally or experientially able to appropriately teach social skills, it is helpful to provide information about resources, developmental progress, and interventions (Semrud-Clikeman & Schafer, 2000).

3. *Michelle Garcia Winner (Center for Social Thinking* – http://www.socialthinking. com) provides training, workshops, and curriculum for social skills training.

4. *The Social Emotional Learning Framework (SELF): A way to enhance understanding and focus interventions, the SELF* was developed by Meryl Lipton, M.D., Ph.D., Director of Rush Neurobehavioral Center in Chicago Illinois and her team. The framework is presented as a possible way to help refocus clinical and research efforts regarding children with NVLD and other brain-based social emotional learning disorders (BB-SELD). Rather than primarily being concerned with delineating differences among BB-SELD children, the SELF, instead, emphasizes their shared difficulties in processing social emotional information. More specifically, the SELF describes (1) a possible set of brain-based social emotional processes; (2) currently available ways to assess social emotional learning strengths and weaknesses; and (3) a variety of strategies for interventions.

5. *Speech therapists* can help NVLD students with both semantic and pragmatic language. An example of such a language program is: *Diamond Social Skills*, created by Susan Diamond, M.A., CCC Speech Pathologist. It provides parents with activities, strategies, and games to help their children develop social skills. It discusses turn taking, topic initiation, language processing, etc. (http://www. diamondlanguage.com).

6. *College Internship Program* – Michael McManmon (http://www. Collegeinternshipprogram.com) offers a residential treatment program providing wrap-around support for college students with NVLD.

7. *Mind Reading: The Interactive Guide to Emotions* (Baron-Cohen, 2004; http:// www.jkp.com/mindreading). This is an interactive program that demonstrates over 400 different human emotions.

8. *Teaching Your Child the Language of Social Success* by Marshal P. Duke, Stephen Nowicki Jr., and Elisabeth A. Martin (1996) is a book/manual for helping children and a follow-up book for adults as well (Nowicki & Duke, 2002) who have difficulty reading or sending nonverbal emotional material (referred to as dyssemia) which works on improving verbal and nonverbal processing skills. There are ideas for working with individuals as well as adapting the principles to the classroom.

9. The School Age Book: It's so much work being your friend: helping children with learning disabilities find social success (Lavoie, 2005).

10. Sitcoms on television – Our clinical experience supports the use of repeated viewing and discussion of comedy and soap opera television shows. The exaggerated emotions portrayed on these shows offer ample opportunity for discussion and increased understanding. Videotaping the child and reviewing the material together are an additional way to address these deficits.

Intellectual Reasoning

Children with NVLD often have difficulty with reasoning, including visual-spatial reasoning and fluid reasoning/novel problem solving.

Interventions

1. *Perceptual Enrichment Program (PEP)* – PEP (Kreidler, 1996) is a cognitive-based developmentally oriented treatment modality based on principles of both child development and cognitive rehabilitation. A trained therapist, most often an occupational therapist, who guides the child's exploration, presents novel, developmentally graded problem-solving tasks using the materials to tailor the task to the child's developmental and remedial needs. Materials include primary

school activities such as mosaic designs, sorting, logic and sequential reasoning tasks that encourage the child to integrate both analytical and gestalt problem-solving strategies.

The Perceptual Enrichment Program, developed in 1982, has some clinical/anecdotal evidence suggesting that it can effect changes in skills thought to be mediated by frontal lobe development in a number of children treated both at California Pacific Medical Center's Child Development Center (CMPC) and by Occupational and Educational Therapists in private practice (Kreidler, 1996). To date, case studies utilizing PEP reveal changes in attention, visual perception, classification, processing speed, and visual-motor integration among a sample of school-aged children treated from 1993 to 1996 at CPMC (Kreidler, 1996). Changes of one to two standard deviations on standardized tests of cognitive processing were seen among students in a preliminary retrospective study (Kreidler, 1996, unpublished manuscript and personal communication). Geographically, the two main areas PEP Associations can be found are in Copenhagen, Denmark and in San Francisco, CA, USA. It has also been reported that the PEP is currently being studied in Boston, MA with MRIs taken before and after PEP treatment by qualified facilitators. Information can be requested by contacting ptheisen@mantraonline.com.

2. *Drawing with Language* (http://www.lblp.com or 800 233-1819) is a structured program developed by Lindamood-Bell to improve visual-spatial skills through their summer programs. Students are taught to visualize a math concept and then learn to draw it.

Academics

Academic interventions are often needed to support children with mathematics, writing, and planning/organization and reading comprehension.

Math – Interventions can consist of direct instruction and therapies, modification of classroom environment, modification of academic load, and scaffolding to support the student's progress in nonaffected areas (Semrud-Clikeman & Fine, 2010). Written calculation was found to be most impaired (Forrest, 2004) suggesting that the mechanics of performing written math (i.e., lining up number columns) is an area of difficulty. Modifications to help with this problem include using graph or column paper to assist with number alignment. Adjustment of the curriculum to include an enriched verbal explanation of the material as opposed to blackboard demonstration only has proven useful, by clinical report. While early number concepts and facts may not necessarily challenge NVLD children, as concepts become more abstract and spatial (e.g., geometry, trigonometry), they may benefit from one-on-one tutoring by a mathematics educator skilled in translating math concepts verbally.

Interventions

1. *On Cloud Nine®* (http://www.lblp.com or 800 233-1819) is a structured program developed by Tuley and Bell (1997), which stimulates the ability to image and verbalize the concepts underlying math processes. Concept and Numeral imagery are integrated with language and applied to math computation and problem solving. There is emphasis on both mathematical reasoning and mathematical computation.
2. *Math from A-Z – Sarah Harris* (sarahha2z@sbcglobal.net). This is a color-coded, well-structured, and sequenced curriculum for basic math skill development. Originally intended as an instructional set of strategies with more verbalization meant to appeal more to girls, the added structure, strategy, and verbalizations could also be helpful to NVLD students.
3. *Making Math Real – David Berg: A Multisensory, Structured Program for Cognitive Development in Mathematics* (http://www.makingmathreal.org/). This program offers multisensory structured methodologies which deliver all instructions via the three processing modalities: visual, auditory, and kinesthetic-motoric. The creators of Making Math Real suppose that students who are struggling experience processing difficulties in either one or more of these processing modalities. They emphasize that best instructional practices require linking all incoming information across the three channels to maximize successful processing.
4. *Math-U-See* (Demi, undated; http://MathUSee.com). This is another multisensory, manipulative-based curriculum for beginning math skills up through pre-Calculus (including Algebra and Geometry). The program includes a series of DVDs and materials to enhance math skills in struggling students. The approach includes:

   1. Explicit Instruction – directly teaches skills for math
   2. Systematic and Cumulative – has a definite logical sequence of concept introduction
   3. Structured – uses step-by-step procedures for introducing, reviewing, and practicing concepts
   4. Multisensory – engages visual, auditory, and kinesthetic channels simultaneously or in rapid succession
   5. Progress Monitoring – uses ongoing progress monitoring with frequent opportunities to reteach

There was one evaluation of the program noted on the website where students receiving special education services in the Albuquerque Public Schools demonstrated significant gains through the implementation of Math-U-See. However, there were no control groups.

Writing – Writing is an often an area of difficulty for children with NVLD. Initially, it is the physical act of writing which forms a barrier to developing writing as a method of effective communication (see the section on fine motor skills in this chapter). Dictation is often recommended for content-based exercises if the child is not able to produce a written product. By allowing the child to continue to grow academically without being held back by production issues, some negative emotionality and lowering of self-esteem may be avoided (Davis & Broitman, 2007). Older students may experience difficulty with organizing their ideas into a cohesive written report. If symptoms of ADHD are present, this type of task can become even more challenging (see section on executive functioning in Chapter 7). Adolescents with NVLD may need more help from adults during this process than do their nonaffected peers.

Reading Comprehension

Interventions

1. *Lindamood-Bell Visualizing and Verbalizing® program* (V/V®) attempts to stimulate the underlying process involved in reading to improve comprehension and to stimulate concept imagery. Individuals may become able to image gestalts that include color and movement. It has been found to improve their language comprehension, reasoning for critical thinking, and expressive language skills in some children. Although there is no research specifically designed for NVLD students, their website does have research documenting the success of this program among children with other learning problems. However, we must be mindful that it was really developed for children with dyslexia rather than NVLD (visit http://www.lblp.com).
2. *Edzyme*™ ("*Educational Enzyme*") model (http://www.individualu.com/) provides one-on-one mentor-tutors who are part of a collaborative student-centric educational team that communicates regularly with parents, schools, therapists to help to a child's progress.
3. There are a number of books written to address students' difficulties with reading comprehension. Books such as *Bringing Words to Life* (Beck, McKeown, & Kucan, 2000), *Vocabulary Development* (Stahl, 1999), and *Improving Reading Comprehension: Research Based Principles and Practices* (Carlisle & Rice, 2002) are good examples. For a more comprehensive list of possible intervention-oriented books, see Martin (2007).

Psychotherapy

Finally, we would like to discuss group and individual psychotherapy, and life coaching as potential interventions for our NVLD clients. Considerable controversy exists regarding the usefulness of these interventions. Research on the treatment of emotional and behavioral disturbances is needed to determine the appropriateness of different therapeutic approaches with this population. To this end, further study may attempt to identify the specific type of therapy that is best suited for individuals with NVLD. Although researchers suggest that insight-oriented therapy may appear to be indicated due to the verbal strengths of individuals with NVLD (Rourke & Tsatsanis, 1996), Schloerb (2005) reminds us that it is important to remember that a high level of verbal output does not equate with abilities in concept forming and problem solving, which are significantly lacking in individuals diagnosed with NVLD. Specifically, she recommends that therapists must explore the ways in which therapy might capitalize on existing linguistic strengths to treat cognitive deficits.

There is a general consensus in the field of learning disabilities that problems persist throughout the lifecycle (Johnson, 1987b; Palombo, 2001) suggesting that therapy may continue to be useful throughout, or at least intermittently. Adults with NVLD have reported that counseling is helpful in dealing with frustration, but Schloerb (2005) suggests that practitioners should also include help for immediate problem solving, rather than only emphasizing the resolution of previous conflicts (Johnson, 1987b).

Due to the highly verbal nature of children with NVLD, the authors believe that therapy is likely to be helpful at least in some circumstances. It would be imperative that the clinicians have familiarity with the particular characteristics of their clients with NVLD, such as their tendency toward concreteness, misinterpretation of pragmatics, difficulty with insight, and need for repeated practice prior to generalization. They should be well informed regarding the success of psychopharmacology with depression and anxiety reduction. The therapist can best function as a life coach providing a safe environment where the child/adult can verbally mediate their concerns and receive practical guidance. In addition, the therapist can use their dynamic understanding to help the child/adult with NVLD mediate developmental milestones and achieve maximum autonomy.

Summary

In this chapter we have offered examples of interventions that are suggested to target key deficits for children with NVLD. We organized them into categories of dysfunction separated into: *motor coordination, visual-spatial/sensory perception, executive functioning, social/emotional deficits, intellectual reasoning,* and *academic programs.* Unfortunately, as there remains no research basis upon which to check the efficacy of these interventions, they are primarily offered for illustrative purposes only. Lastly, we discussed the use of psychotherapy for children with NVLD. In Chapter 12 we offer some concluding remarks.

Chapter 12
Final Thoughts

In this chapter we would like to share our thinking regarding the most important concepts we hoped to cover in this book. We believe that children with NVLD can successfully learn and lead productive lives despite their particularly unusual set of strengths and difficulties. They will need the considerable help of their families and many different practitioners throughout their lives. All clinicians have to understand and be able to refer to the other team members to make sure all aspects of the child are understood. It is vital to avoid getting trapped by dilemmas like that of the blind men and the elephant, each mistakenly thinking they have whole story. We strongly recommend a collaborative model for evaluation, understanding, intervention, and follow up. A child with NVLD may enter the system at many different points in his or her life. Which practitioner they meet with first will depend on the age and developmental level of the children. It is essential that the parents, teachers, and occupational therapists talk to the speech pathologist and psychiatrists/psychologists. These children force professionals to look and/or reach outside our traditional view.

We believe that although children with NVLD share some characteristics with children who are diagnosed with Asperger's, the research remains divided and the answer is not yet clear. We believe there are enough differences between the two that NVLD should be a separate diagnostic category with its own subtypes. We believe that this will allow the treatment focus to be more comprehensive and accurate. While further research will answer some important current questions, we believe that our four-part model is an extremely useful heuristic tool which can be used to guide assessment and intervention.

In terms of the current zeitgeist in education around the Response to Intervention (RTI) focus, our clinical experience suggests that RTI alone will not work as well for children with NVLD as say their learning-disabled counterparts with dyslexia, because current data suggest that most of the students with dyslexia struggle with what has become known as a "phonological core deficit" (Christo, Davis, & Brock, 2009) which can be identified more readily with a single focus screening battery and can be handled with a more focused intervention. As we have stated throughout the book, students with NVLD present with a variety of potential symptoms, and clinicians need to become more adept at knowing that if there is one symptom

J.M. Davis and J. Broitman, *Nonverbal Learning Disabilities in Children:*
Bridging the Gap Between Science and Practice, DOI 10.1007/978-1-4419-8213-1_12,
© Springer Science+Business Media, LLC 2011

which might fit with an NVLD pattern, other symptoms should be explored to insure a comprehensive treatment program.

Also, these children are very likely to need case management, support, and intervention throughout their school careers. They may well also receive support from other professionals in the community so again collaboration/consultation will be needed.

Parents will need a lot of support to sort out and through the different treatment options for their child. It is counterproductive to overload a child with too much help at once. One will have to prioritize and sequence which symptom to focus on at a specific time. We recommend addressing the specific impairment that is currently most in danger of damaging the child's self-esteem. In addition we suggest that families support a positive skill stemming from an area of the child's strength at the same time as arranging a tutor for an area of weakness. Drama, for example, often plays to the strengths of children with NVLD. We encourage practitioners to use the child's interests as a focus for interventions. We want to stress that the further import of a comprehensive evaluation is to take baselines in all relevant areas from which to document changes (or not) following interventions. One can also use these measures to help decide termination issues as well.

Finally, we strongly suggest that one provides scaffolding for success and reduce support upon success. Many professionals are overly concerned about creating dependency and thwarting the child's independence. It is our experience that with structure and support in place children with NVLD are motivated to, and can, become highly independent. They will however need to be able to return to their safe base for guidance when faced with challenging novel experiences. Understanding their ongoing needs is crucial, without pathologizing their needs for assistance.

We hope that this book will offer assistance in the assessment and treatment of children with NVLD. We believe that with early intervention and support children with NVLD can lead fulfilling successful lives. Their unique perspectives allow them the potential to make significant original contributions. This process has been beautifully described by a young man with NVLD with whom we have worked with: "It's like climbing a spiral staircase. At first it feels as though you are just going around and around in the same place. But slowly and surely, if you just continue on you go up a step, and then another, till you accomplish your goal." We believe his words succinctly capture our observations. You will hear directly from this remarkable young man next in the afterthoughts.

Afterword

Brett Mills

I know both the authors of this book quite well and have been on the receiving end of a great deal of the interventions that they discuss. I hope that by sharing some of my personal experience I will help drive home why it is so important that one treats a case like mine with caution, and help the reader to take this book's conclusion to heart. It can be overwhelming to think about the large task that faces anyone working with or trying to overcome an NVLD. I like to think that one's frame of mind has a great deal of influence on one's ability to overcome any obstacle. To deal with my NVLD I had to embrace the fact that life is a process. I had to learn that nothing is ever finished and that what I was ultimately working toward was the right to keep pursuing more.

The reason why this is so important to realize is that a great deal of this "process" can feel a lot like banging your head against a brick wall over and over again. To be good at it, you need to be able to relish small victories and have enough self-respect and confidence to know how to get back up and keep trying even when it feels impossible. All of this is easier said than done, and all that I can say is that whatever ability I have to accomplish any of this has exists because of the encouragement of my mother. She both pushed and nurtured me so that I could persevere in the face of a relatively small amount of understanding.

The great frustration that comes with an NVLD (and probably any learning disability) is that you do not feel like you are missing something. It does not feel like you have a disorder; the world just does not make a lot of sense. It is hard to reconcile why things that are so easy for others to grasp seem unattainable to me. Once I was able to get myself into a mindset that made it okay for me to enjoy the process, I was able to relax about the things which seemed mind-numbingly difficult. I had convinced myself that by working hard and slowly moving along, everything would get worked out, and I would be a fully functioning adult when the time came.

I can remember having this mindset all the way back to when I had trouble learning to tie my shoes (and by the way I am talking about having trouble doing this at age nine or ten, not six or seven). The point is that I was given an environment and a team of people who assured me that I would be fine. This allowed me to focus on the things that would propel me forward. If a great deal of shame were associated with these issues (and there was some – it is inevitable), I imagine that I would have

J.M. Davis and J. Broitman, *Nonverbal Learning Disabilities in Children:*
Bridging the Gap Between Science and Practice, DOI 10.1007/978-1-4419-8213-1,
© Springer Science+Business Media, LLC 2011

shut down. This would have kept me from having the emotional energy to develop my own process.

The type of work that is required is exhausting, and I think that it is very hard for an observer be sure that the process someone with NVLD has decided to follow is yielding any kind of positive result. Some of the most useful aids has come from the most unlikely places: TV sitcoms (which gave me my first window into under-standing social interaction), juggling (which gave me self-confidence and had a major effect on my visual-spatial processing), and computer uses like Facebook (which taught me to type). I remember being on what felt like the receiving end of a lot of frustration, because people would feel like they had shown me how to do something and I had yet to even begin to grasp it.

Recently, in a totally different context, I heard a metaphor that I think is very applicable to the experience of someone with NVLD. Making breakthroughs in your personal struggle with NVLD is a lot like walking up a spiral staircase very slowly. It will feel like you are going around in circles, but what is actually happen-ing is that you are revisiting something from one level above where you were the last time the issue made itself known. Things feel repetitive and redundant, but ultimately small victories become large ones and you are doing things that you never thought possible.

I was confronted with my feelings about process when it came time to start my freshman year of college. It was the first time I had to look over the previous 18 years of my life and really think about the result. I had to ask myself where I had gotten, and whether or not I was finally ready to just count myself amongst the others and let my LD issues just wash into the background. I was on the fence as to whether or not I wanted to inform my professors of my situation. My mother strongly urged me to meet with my college Learning Specialist, if for no other reason than to have a file in case something came up and I needed any sort of accommodation.

My meeting with my school's specialist was the first time in my life that I had ever heard anyone read me my file. I do not remember everything that she read, but one phrase did stick out to me: "writing is a slow and laborious process." I was a little taken aback by this because math was the thing that I was supposed to be "bad" at. The learning specialist also seemed confused and avoided (but clearly communicated) the question that I myself was beginning to ask myself, which was "how did you end up here?" It is important to note that the college I attend is rea-sonably prestigious and is above all else known for making its students write like there is no tomorrow. The specialist did not know what to do with the information in my file, and that meeting was the first and last time that she and I interacted.

After leaving her office I made the choice to not tell any of my professors about my learning disability. The meeting with the specialist was a very valuable experi-ence for me because I realized I no longer had a gauge on where I was, neurologically. If I were to attempt to describe my circumstance to a professor, I was not sure what I would say. It seemed that even if I did communicate some-thing, that something would not be an accurate representation of the truth and would not necessarily serve as an asset. What I had heard from my file did not ring true with the student that I had thought I had become. I decided that it would be valuable to see what it would look like if I were evaluated on what I could produce, rather than what I was producing given a handicap.

At the end of the year I reached the conclusion that I do indeed still have a learning disability. It was evident in my professors' responses to my work that they saw a discrepancy between what I could produce verbally and what actually made its way on to a page. I was even chastised somewhat harshly for it. I received the occasional "if only you put a little more attention or effort into this paper you could realize your full potential." The fact of the matter is that I was spread as thin as I could have been, and that what had they received was as good as they were going to get. To the credit of my professors, I had friends who produced work at the quality that I did who did not work nearly as hard as I did. The point is that the professors were not wrong to notice a discrepancy. There was no way for them to know how or why it was occurring, and in other cases their response may have proved useful.

The most insulting and hurtful thing that you can say to someone with a learning disorder is that they are lazy or should work harder. You have no idea how hard they are working, and those words will inspire nothing. Tough love is misplaced in this kind of a situation. I can only imagine the kind of frustration that I have put many a teacher through, and yet I think that the ones who served me best are the ones who displayed patience and understanding. They created a safe environment where I could express confusion and frustration. If I encountered a situation where I felt judged, I usually became too scared to speak up and just let myself get further and further behind while just nodding "yes" to everything that the teacher said.

In spite of some suffering along the way I actually finished out my first year with a good deal of success and excellent grades. The year taught me that the process is not over. I will not ever be able to stop and say "okay, here we are, this is the day that the work was preparing me for." I will always have a learning disability, and it will always keep me from fitting into any kind of normative category. I will continue to encounter people who do not understand my disability, but I have reached a place internally where it is okay with me to not always be perfectly understood. When it matters I will make whatever needs to be known made known, but I think that continuing to be an adult in the process requires that I pick and choose which battles to fight, as you really cannot win them all. I have finally reached a place where I can say that I have overcome enough to decide what to overcome next and what to let go. I think that once the next step is no longer clear, you will know that you have really accomplished something.

Appendix

The following is a list of potentially useful websites. *The authors do not endorse or recommend any of them but offer the list as a resource.*

504 Plan Information	http://www.burltwpsch.org/
Advocacy	http://www.conductdisorders.com
American Hyperlexia Association	http://www.hyperlexia.org
American Speech-Language- Hearing Association (ASHA)	http://www.asha.org
Anxiety Disorders Association of America (ADAA)	http://www.asha.org
Anxiety	http://www.nimh.nih.gov/anxiety
Aspen	http://www.AspenNJ.org
Asperger's	http://www.asperger.org/
Assistive Technology and LD	http://www.ldresources.com
Assistive Technology	http://www.assistivetech.com
Association on Higher Education and Disability (AHEAD)	http://www.ahead.org
Books on Tape Talking Book Library – California	http://www.library.ca.gov/html/pubser05.html
Books on Tape: Recording for the Blind and Dyslexic	http://www.rfbd.org/
Brain Connection	http://www.brainconnection.com
Center for Speech and Language Disorders	http://www.csld.org
Center for Speech and Language Disorders	http://www.csld.org
Central Auditory Processing Disorder CAPD	http://kidshealth.org/parent/healthy/central_auditory.html
Children and Adults with Attention Deficit/ Hyperactivity Disorder (CHADD)	http://www.chadd.org
Children with Spina Bifida, a Resource Page for Parents	http://www.waisman.wisc.edu/~rowley/sb-kids/
Conduct Disorders	http://www.conductdisorders.com/

Consortium FOR Citizens WITH Disabilities	http://www.c-c-d.org/
Council for Learning Disabilities	http://www.cldinternational.org
Council of Parent Attorneys and Advocates	http://www.copaa.net
Dutch NLD Site	http://www.geocities.com/Athens/Academy/1644/
Dyspraxia Article	http://www.allhealth.com/childrens/qa/0,4801,1620_121375,00.html
Dyspraxia Foundation	http://www.emmbrook.demon.co.uk/dysprax/homepage.htm
Educational Resources Information Center (ERIC)	http://www.eric.ed.gov
Educational Therapy's website	http://www.edtherapy.com/students/htm
Excellent Literature, Homework Information	http://www.embracingthechild.com (*look in the tutor section for literature*)
Facts for Families... About Psychiatric Disorders Affecting Children and Adults	http://www.aacap.org/web/aacap/factsFam/
Free Advocacy for Parents	http://www.amicusforchildren.org
Gifted and LD	http://www.uniquelygifted.org
Gifted and LD	http://www.uniquelygifted.org
Good Basic Information+Self Advocacy info	http://www.LDinfo.com
Handwriting	http://www.BFHhandwriting.com
Hoagies' Gifted Education Page	http://www.hoagiesgifted.org/
Hyperlexia	http://www.hyperlexia.org/
IDEA Information	http://www.ideapractices.org/docs/ideadepot/userguide.htm #guidepurpose
IEP Information	http://www.cesa7.k12.wi.us/sped/
IEP Information	http://www.awesomelibrary.org/Library/Special_Education/Individualized_Education_Plans/Individualized_Education_Plans.html
IEP/advocacy Information	http://www.wrightslaw.com
Interactive Metronome	http://www.interactivemetronome.com./
ISER – internet special education resources	http://www.iser.com
LD OnLine	http://www.ldonline.org/
LD On Line Social Skills with Rick Lavoie	http://ldonline.org/ld_indepth/social_skills/lavoie_quest.html
LD Online	http://www.ldonline.org
LD Pride Online	http://www.ldpride.net
Learning Disabilities Association of America	http://www.ldanatl.org
Learning Disabilities Association of America, California	http://www.ldaca.org
Lisa Marti's Nonverbal Learning Disability Cyber Advocacy and Support Group	http://www.geocities.com/Athens/Pantheon/3433
Literature, Homework Information	http://www.embracingthechild.com (*look in the tutor section for literature*)
Margaret Kay, PhD	http://www.margaretkay.com

Matrix	http://www.matrixparents.org/faq.html
Mind Steps Career Software	http://www.mind-steps.com
Misunderstood Minds	http://www.pbs.org/misunderstoodminds
National Center for Learning Disabilities	http://www.ncld.org
National Information Center for Children/Youth with Disabilities	http://www.nichcy.org/
National Institute of Neurological Disorders & Stroke	http://www.ninds.nih.gov/
Nerd World	http://www.nerdworld.com
NLD Articles	http://laran.waisman.wisc.edu/fv/www/lib_nvld.html#Articles
NLD On the Web	http://www.nldontheweb.org/
NLDA	http://www.nlda.org
NLDA, Nonverbal Learning Disorders Association	NLDResources@aol.com, http://www.nlda.org/
NLDline	http://www.nlda.org/
NLDontheweb.org	http://www.NLDontheweb.org/
Nonverbal Dictionary (Center for Nonverbal Studies)	http://members.aol.com/nonverbal2/index.htm
Noonan Syndrome	http://noonansyndrome.org
OASIS	http://www.udel.edu/bkirby/asperger/
Obsessive Compulsive Disorder (OCD)	http://www.ocdawareness.com/
Online Asperger Syndrome Information and Support (O.A.S.I.S.)	http://www.udel.edu/bkirby/asperger
Out-of-Sync Child Webpage	http://www.comeunity.com/disability/sensory_integration/bksync.html
Parent to Parent Support	http://www.NPPSIS.org
Parents and Educators Resource Center	http://www.perc-schwabfdn.org
Parents of Gifted/Learning Disabled Children	http://www.geocities.com/Athens/1105/gtld.html
Pathways to Technology	pathwaystotechnology.org
Recording for the Blind & Dyslexic (RFB&D)	http://www.rfbd.org
Rondalyn Whitney's website	http://www.thelighthouseproject.com
Rush Neurobehavioral Center	http://www.rush.edu/rnbc
Sensory Integration Resource Network	http://www.sinetwork.org/
SOS – Executive Function	http://www.sos4students.com
Special Ed Advocacy	http://www.reedmartin.com/
Special Ed Links	http://alpha.fdu.edu/~dumont/extended_links.htm
Special Ed News (updated weekly)	http://www.specialednews.com/
Special Needs online Newsletter	*Subscribe*: special-needs-books-subscribe@onelist.com, http://home.freeuk.net/theadhdgazette
Speech and Language Software	http://www.locutour.com/

Spirited Kids Family Resource Center	http://network54.com/Realm/Spirited_Kids
Stern Center for Language and Learning	http://sterncenter.org
Stern Center, Williston, Vermont	http://www.sterncenter.org
Struggling Teens	http://www.strugglingteens.com/
TAWK	http://www.nldsupport.org.
Tera Kirk: (an NLD teenager's great website)	http://www.geocities.com/HotSprings/Spa/7262
Tony Attwood	http://www.tonyattwood.com
Website for Learning Disabilities	http://www.abilityhub.com
Wrightslaw	http://www.wrightslaw.com
Yale Study	http://info.med.yale.edu/chldstdy/research.htm

Alternative Methods/Interventions/Programs

(not tested or recommended by authors!!)

http://icdl.com/forparentsbyparents/sensoryprocessing/sensorycontent.htm

Dalcroze Eurhythmics uses movement and music, rhythmic responses, and social integration.

NeuroNet a lot of balancing, following a rhythm (we use metronome), throwing, catching, counting, naming, visual tracing, controlling body movements… – and integrating of all of the above

The Alexander Technique

Yoga and a class at the local gym called Neuro-muscular Integrative Action (NIA) which is a form of low impact aerobics, dance and martial arts balance exercises

Improv workshops

EMDR (Eye Movement Desensitization and Reprocessing) and BIOLATERAL TAPES

Balametrics

Interactive Metronome

Brain Gym

Sensory Learning – Bolles Method The treatment retrains the brain to coordinate and send information from mind to body.

http://neuroacoustics.com/

http://www.mentalskills.com

Neurobiofeedback

References

Achenbach, T. T. (1985). *Assessment and taxonomy of child and adolescent psychology* (Developmental clinical psychology and psychiatry, Vol. 3). Beverly Hills, CA: Sage.

Achenbach, T. T. (2001a). *The child behavior checklist*. Burlington, VT: ASEBA.

Achenbach, T. T. (2001b). *The teacher report form*. Burlington, VT: ASEBA.

Achenbach, T., & Edelbrock, I. (1983). *The child behavior checklist-Revised*. Burlington, VT: Queen City Printers.

Adams, W., & Sheslow, D. (1995). *Wide range assessment of visual motor abilities*. Wilmington, DE: Wide Range.

Ahern, C. A., & de Kirby, K. (in press). Beyond individual differences: Organizing processes, information overload, and classroom learning. (Springer in press)

Allen, K. (1998). *Star shaped pegs, square holes: Nonverbal learning disorders and the growing up years*. Livermore, CA: Good Enough Books.

Amaral, D. G., Schumann, C. M., & Nordahl, C. W. (2008). Neuroanatomy of autism. *Trends in Neurosciences, 31*, 137–145.

American Psychiatric Association. (2000). *Diagnostic and statistical manual of mental disorders* (4th ed.). Washington, DC: American Psychiatric Association. Text Revision.

Anderson, P., & Rourke, B. P. (1995). Williams syndrome. In B. P. Rourke (Ed.), *Syndrome of nonverbal learning disabilities: Neurodevelopmental manifestations* (pp. 138–170). New York: Guilford Press.

Antshel, K., & Guy-Ronald, J. (2006). Maternal stress in nonverbal learning disorder. *Journal of Learning Disability, 39*(3), 194–205.

Antshel, K., & Khan, F. M. (2008). Is there an increased familial prevalence of psychopathology in children with nonverbal learning disorders? *Journal of Learning Disabilities, 41*, 208–217.

Ashtari, M., Kumra, S., Bhaskar, S., Clarke, T., Thaden, E., Cervellione, K., et al. (2005). Attention-deficit/hyperactivity disorder: A preliminary diffusion tensor imaging study. *Biological Psychiatry, 57*(5), 448–455.

Attwood, T. (2007). *The complete guide to Asperger's syndrome*. London: Jessica Kingsley Publishers.

Ayres, J. (1994). *Sensory integration and learning disorders*. Los Angeles: Western Psychological Services.

Badian, N. A., & Ghubilikian, M. (1983). The personal–social characteristics of children with poor mathematical computation skills. *Journal of Learning Disabilities, 16*, 154–157.

Bannatyne, A. (1974). Diagnosis: A note on categorization of the WISC scaled scores. *Journal of Learning Disabilities, 7*, 272–274.

Barkley, R. A. (1997). *Defiant children* (2nd ed.). New York: Guilford.

Barnhill, G., Hagiwara, T., Myles, B. S., & Simpson, R. L. (2000). Asperger syndrome. *Focus on autism and other developmental disabilities, 15*(3), 146–153.

Baron-Cohen, S. (1997). *Mindblindness an essay on autism and theory of mind*. Cambridge, MA: MIT press.

Barton, J., Mooney, P., & Prasad, S. (2005). Atomoxetine hydrochloride and executive function in children with attention-deficit/hyperactivity disorder. *Journal of Child and Adolescent Psychopharmacology, 15*(2), 147–149.

Bearden, C. E., Woodin, M. F., Wang, P. P., Moss, E., McDonald-McGinn, D., Zackai, E., et al. (2001). The neurocognitive pheno-type of the 22q11.2 deletion syndrome: Selective deficit in visual-spatial memory. *Journal of Clinical and Experimental Neuropsychology, 18*, 447–464.

Beck, I. L., McKeown, M. G., & Kucan, L. (2000). *Bringing words to life: Robust vocabulary instruction*. New York: Guilford.

Beery, K. E., Buktenica, N. A., & Beery, N. A. (2006). *The visual-motor integration test* (5th ed.). Austin, TX: Pro-Ed.

Bender, W. N., & Golden, L. B. (1990). Subtypes of students with learning disabilities as derived from cognitive, academic, behavioral, and self-concept measures. *Learning Disability Quarterly, 13*, 183–194.

Bender, W. N., Rosenkrans, C. B., & Crane, M.-K. (1999). Stress, depression, and suicide among students with learning disabilities: Assessing the risk. *Learning Disability Quarterly, 22*(2), 143–156.

Bender, W. N., & Shores, C. (Eds.). (2007). *Response to intervention: A practical guide for every teacher*. Thousand Oaks, CA: Council for Exceptional Children and Crown Press.

Benton, A. L., Sivan, A. B., Hamsher, K., Varney, N. R., & Spreen, O. (1983). *Judgement of line orientation*. New York: Oxford University Press.

Benton, A. L., Varney, N. R., & Hamsher, K. (1978). Visuospatial judgment: A clinical test. *Archives of Neurology, 35*, 364–367.

Berninger, V. W. (2007). *Process assessment of the learner* (2nd ed.). San Antonio, TX: Harcourt Assessments.

Berninger, V. W., & Richards, T. L. (2002). *Brain literacy for educators and psychologists*. New York: Elsevier Science.

Berninger, V. W., & Richards, T. L. (2002). *Brain literacy for educators and psychologists*. San Diego, CA: Elsevier Science.

Berquin, P. C., Giedd, J. N., Jacobsen, L. K., Hamburger, S. D., Krain, A. L., Rapoport, J. L., et al. (1998). Cerebellum in attention-deficit hyperactivity disorder: A morphometric MRI study. *Neurology, 50*(4), 1087–1093.

Bigler, E. (1989). On the neuropsychology of suicide. *Journal of Learning Disabilities, 22*, 180–185.

Bishop, D. (2000). Pragmatic language impairment: A correlate of SLI, a distinct subgroup, or part of the autistic continuum. In D. Bishop & L. Leonard (Eds.), *Speech and language impairments in children: Causes, characteristics, intervention, and outcome* (pp. 99–113). Hove, East Sussex, UK: Psychology Press.

Blim, L. M. (2002). Private communication.

Bloom, L. (1988). What is language? In M. Lahey (Ed.), *Language disorders and language development* (pp. 1–19). New York: MacMillan Publishing.

Bos, C. S., & Van Reusen, A. K. (1991). Academic interventions with learning disabled students: A cognitive/metacognitive approach. In J. Obrzut & G. W. Hynd (Eds.), *Neuropsychological foundations of learning disabilities* (pp. 659–684). Orlando, FL: Academic Press.

Brickenkamp, R., & Zillmer, E. A. (1998). *d2 test of attention*. Seattle, WA: Hogrefe and Huber Publishers.

Brooks, R. (1991). *The self-esteem teacher*. Loveland, OH: Treehaus Communications.

Brooks, R. (2001). *Raising resilient children*. New York: McGraw-Hill.

Brouwers, P., van der Vlugt, H., Moss, H., Wolters, P., & Pizzo, P. (1995). White matter changes on CT brain scan are associated with neurobehavioral dysfunction in children with symptomatic HIV disease. *Child Neuropsychology, 1*(2), 93–105.

Brown, T. E. (2000). Emerging understandings of attention-deficit disorders and comorbidities. In T. E. Brown (Ed.), *Attention-deficit disorders and comorbidities in children, adolescents, and adults*. Washington, DC: American Psychiatric Press.

Brown, J. I., Fischo, V. V., & Hanna, G. S. (1993). *Nelson-Denny reading test*. Rolling Meadows, IL: Riverside Publishing.

Bruck, M. (1986). Social and emotional adjustments of learning disabled children: A review of the issues. In S. J. Ceci (Ed.), *Handbook of cognitive, social, and neuropsychological aspects of learning disabilities* (Vol. 1, pp. 361–380). Hillsdale, NJ: Lawrence Erlbaum.

Brumback, R. A. (1985). Wechsler performance IQ deficit in depression in children. *Perceptual and Motor Skills, 61*, 331–335. 1992-72720-001.

Brumback, R. A., Harper, C. R., & Weinberg, W. A. (1996). Nonverbal learning disabilities, Asperger's syndrome, pervasive developmental disorder – should we care? *Journal of Child Neurology, 11*, 427–429.

Brumback, R. A. (1985). Wechsler performance IQ deficit in depression in children. *Perceptual and Motor Skills, 61*, 331–335. 1992-72720-001.

Bryan, K. L., & Hale, J. B. (2001). Differential effects of left and right hemisphere accidents on language competency. *Journal of the International Neuropsychological Society, 7*, 655–664.

Buchanan, L., Pavlovic, J., & Rovet, J. (1998). A reexamination of the visuospatial deficit in Turner syndrome: Contributions of working memory. *Developmental Neuropsychology Special Issue: Gonadal Hormones and Sex Differences in Behavior, 14*, 341–367.

Butler, M. G., & Meaney, F. J. (Eds.). (2005). *Genetics of developmental disabilities*. Philadelphia: Taylor & Francis.

Carey, M. E., Barakat, L. P., Foley, B., Gyato, K., & Phillips, P. C. (2001). Neuropsychological functioning and social functioning of survivors of pediatric brain tumors: Evidence of nonverbal learning disability. *Child Neuropsychology, 7*(4), 265–272.

Carey, M. E., Haut, M. W., Reminger, S. L., Hutter, J. J., Theilmann, R., & Kaemingk, K. L. (2008). Reduced frontal white matter volume in long-term childhood leukemia survivors: A voxel-based morphometry study. *American Journal of Neuroradiology, 29*, 792–797.

Carlisle, J. F., & Rice, M. S. (2002). *Improving reading comprehension: Research-based principles and practices*. Baltimore, MD: York Press.

Carlson, C., & Christenson, S. (2005). Evidence-based parent and family interventions in school psychology: Overview and procedures. *School Psychology Quarterly, 20*, 345–351.

Carrow-Woodfolk, E. (1999). *Comprehensive assessment of spoken language*. Circle Pines, MN: American Guidance Service.

Carrow-Woodfolk, E. (1995). *Oral and written language scales*. Austin, TX: Pro-Ed.

Casey, J. E., & Rourke, B. P. (1991). Construct validation of the nonverbal learning disabilities syndrome and model. In B. P. Rourke (Ed.), *Neuropsychological validation of learning disability subtypes* (pp. 271–292). New York: Guilford Press.

Casey, J. E., Rourke, B. P., & Picard, E. M. (1991). Syndrome of nonverbal learning disabilities: Age differences in neuropsychological, academic and socioemotional functioning. *Development and Psychopathology, 3*, 331–347.

Cederlund, M., & Gillberg, C. (2004). One hundred boys with Asperger syndrome. A clinical study of background and associated factors. *Developmental Medicine and Child Neurology, 46*, 652–660.

Christo, C., Davis, J., & Brock, S. (2009). *Identifying, assessing, and treating dyslexia at school*. New York: Springer.

Cohen, M. S. (1997). *Children's memory scale*. San Antonio, TX: Harcourt Publishing Company.

Conners, C. K. (2000). *Conners' continuous performance test (CPT-II)*. North Tonawanda, NY: Multi-Health Systems.

Conners, C. K. (2008). *Conners' child behavior rating scale*. North Tonawanda, NY: Multi-Health Systems.

Connolly, A. J. (2007). *KeyMath-3 diagnostic assessment*. Bloomington, MN: Pearson Assessments.

Connolly, A. J. (2007). *Key math- 3: Diagnostic assessment*. San Antonio, TX: Pearson.

Cope, N., Harold, D., Hill, G., Moskvina, V., Stevenson, J., Holmans, P., et al. (2005). Strong evidence that KIAA0319 on chromosome 6p is a susceptibility gene for developmental dyslexia. *American Journal of Human Genetics, 76*, 581–591.

Cornoldi, C., Rigoni, F., Tressoldi, P. E., & Vio, C. (1999). Imagery deficits in nonverbal learning disabilities. *Journal of Learning Disabilities, 32*, 48–57.

Cornoldi, C., Vecchia, R. D., & Tressoldi, P. E. (1995). Visuo-spatial working memory limitations in low visuo-spatial high verbal intelligence children. *Journal of Child Psychology and Psychiatry, 36*(6), 1053–1064.

Cornoldi, C., Venneri, A., Marconato, F., Molin, A., & Montinari, C. (2003). A rapid screening measure for the identification of visuospatial learning disability in schools. *Journal of Learning Disabilities, 36*(4), 299–306.

Corporation, P. (2002). *Wechsler individual achievement test II*. San Antonio, TX: Psychological Corporation.

Croonenberghs, J., Spaas, K., Wauters, A., Verkerk, R., Scharpe, S., Deboutte, D., et al. (2008). Faulty serotonin-DHEA interactions in autism: Results of the 5-hydroxytryptophan challenge test. *Neuro Endocrinology Letters, 29*, 385–390.

Crovetti, A. B. (1998). *Nonverbal learning disabilities and discourse comprehension: Factors related to level of understanding*. Unpublished doctoral dissertation, University of California, Berkeley.

Davis, J., & Broitman, J. (2006). A brief overview of nonverbal learning disorders. *The Educational Therapist, 27*(3), 5–10.

Davis, J., & Broitman, J. (2007). Nonverbal learning disabilities: Models of proposed subtypes, Part II. *The Educational Therapist, 27*(4), 5–10.

Davis, J., & Broitman, J. (2008). *Nonverbal learning disabilities: Diagnosis and history*. Paper presented at the International Neuropsychological Society.

Dean, R. S., & Woodcock, R. W. (2003). *Dean-Woodcock neuropsychological battery*. Itasca, IL: Riverside Publishing.

DeFries, J. C., McGuffin, P., McClearn, G. E., & Plomin, R. (2001). *Behavioural genetics* (4th ed.). New York: Worth Publishers.

DeFries, J. C., Olson, R. K., Pennington, B. F., & Smith, S. D. (1991). The Colorado reading project: An update. In D. Duane & D. B. Gray (Eds.), *The reading brain: The biological basis of dyslexia* (pp. 53–87). Parkton, MD: York Press.

Del Dotto, J. E., Fisk, J. L., McFadden, G. T., & Rourke, B. P. (1991). Developmental analysis of children/adolescents with nonverbal learning disabilities: Long-term impact on personality adjustment and patterns of adaptive functioning. In B. P. Rourke (Ed.), *Neuropsychological validation of learning disability subtypes* (pp. 293–308). New York: Guilford Press.

Delis, D. C., Kaplan, E., & Kramer, J. H. (2001). *Delis-Kaplan executive functioning system: Examiner's manual*. San Antonio, TX: The Psychological Corporation.

Delis, D. C., Kramer, J. H., Kaplan, E., & Ober, B. (1994). *California verbal learning test, children's version*. San Antonio, TX: The Psychological Corporation.

DeLuca, J. W., Rourke, B. P., & Del Dotto, J. E. (1991). Subtypes of arithmetic-disabled children: Cognitive and personality dimensions. In B. P. Rourke (Ed.), *Neuropsychological validation of learning disability subtypes* (pp. 180–219). New York: Guilford Press.

Denckla, M. B. (1991). Academic and extracurricular aspects of nonverbal learning disabilities. *Psychiatric Annals, 21*, 717–724.

Denckla, M. B. (1979). Childhood learning disabilities. In K. M. Heilman & E. Valenstein (Eds.), *Clinical neuropsychology* (pp. 535–573). New York: Oxford University Press.

Denckla, M. B. (2000). Learning disabilities and attention-deficit/hyperactivity disorder in adults: Overlap with executive dysfunction. In T. E. Brown (Ed.), *Attention deficit disorders and comorbidities in children, adolescents, and adults* (pp. 297–318). Washington, DC: American Psychiatric Press.

Deuel, R. K. (1995). Developmental dysgraphia and motor skills disorders. *Journal of Child Neurology, 10*(Suppl. 1), S6–S7.

Deutsch, G. K., Dougherty, R. F., Bammer, R., Siok, W. T., Gabrieli, J. D. E., & Wandell, B. (2005). Children's reading performance is correlated with white matter structure measured by tensor imaging. *Cortex: A Journal Devoted to the Study of the Nervous System and Behavior, 41*(3), 354–363.

Dorfman, C. (2000). *Social language and theory of mind in children with nonverbal learning disability*. Unpublished doctoral dissertation, University of California, Berkeley.

Draganski, B., Gaser, C., Busch, V., Schuierer, G., Bogdahn, U., & May, A. (2004). Neuroplasticity: Changes in grey matter induced by training. *Nature, 427*, 311–312.

Drummond, C. R., Ahmad, S. A., & Rourke, B. P. (2005). Rules for the classification of younger children with nonverbal learning disabilities and basic phonological processing disabilities. *Archives of Clinical Neuropsychology, 20*, 171–182.

Duane, D. D. (1991). Neurobiological issues in dyslexia. In M. Snowling & M. Thomson (Eds.), *Dyslexia: Integrating theory and practice* (pp. 21–30). London: Whurr.

Durand, M. D., Hulme, C., Larkin, R., & Snowling, M. (2005). The cognitive foundations of reading and arithmetic skills in 7- to 10-year olds. *Journal of Experimental Child Psychology, 91*, 113–136.

Eckert, M. A., Leonard, C. M., Richards, T. L., Aylward, E. H., Thomson, J., & Berninger, V. W. (2003). Anatomical correlates of dyslexia: Frontal and cerebellar findings. *Brain, J26*(2), 482–494.

Edmonson, B., DeJung, J., Leland, H., & Leach, E. (1974). *The test of social inference*. New York: Educational Activities.

Elliott, C. D. (2007). *Differential abilities scale II*. San Antonio, TX: Pearson Education.

Epstein, M. H. (2004). *Behavioral and emotional rating scale (BERS-2)* (2nd ed.). Austin, TX: Pro-Ed.

Fast, Y. (2004). *Individuals with Asperger syndrome or nonverbal learning disability: Stories and strategies*. London: Jessica Kingsley, Publishers.

Feifer, S. G. (2008). Integrating response to intervention (RTI) with neuropsychology: A scientific approach to reading. *Psychology in the Schools, 45*(9), 812–825.

Fine, J. G., Semrud-Clikeman, M., Bledsoe, J., & Hasson, R. (2010). *Meta-analysis of the NVLD empirical literature: Scientific rigor of extant research*. San Diego, CA: American Psychological Association Annual Meeting.

Fine, J. G., Semrud-Clikeman, M., Butcher, B., Walkowiak, J. (2008). Brief report: Attention effect on a measure of social perception. *Journal of Autism and Developmental Disorders, 38*, 1797–1802.

Fine, J. G., & Semrud-Clikeman, M. (2010). Nonverbal learning disabilities: Assessment and intervention. In A. S. Davis (Ed.), *Handbook of pediatric neuropsychology*. Cambridge, UK: Cambridge University Press.

Fine, J. G., Semrud-Clikeman, M., & Bledsoe, (2010). *A critical review of the literature on NVLD as a developmental disorder*. Paper presented at the annual meeting of the American Psychological Association, San Diego, CA.

Fisher, S. E., Francks, C., McCracken, J. T., McGough, J. J., Marlow, A. J., MacPhie, I. L., et al. (2002). A genomewide scan for loci involved in attention-deficit/hyperactivity disorder. *American Journal of Medical Genetics, 70*, 1183–1196.

Flanagan, D. P., Ortiz, S. O., & Alfonso, V. C. (2007). *Essentials of cross-battery assessment* (2nd ed.). Hoboken, NJ: Wiley.

Fletcher, J. M. (1985). External validation of learning disability typologies. In B. P. Rourke (Ed.), *Neuropsychology of learning disabilities: Essentials of subtype analysis* (pp. 187–211). New York: Guilford Press.

Fletcher, J. M. (1989). Nonverbal learning disabilities and suicide: Classification leads to prevention. *Journal of Learning Disabilities, 22*(3), 176–179.

Fletcher-Janzen, E., & Reynolds, C. R. (Eds.). (2008). *Neuropsychological perspectives on learning disabilities in the era of RTI: Recommendations for diagnosis and intervention*. Hoboken, NJ: Wiley.

Forrest, B. (2004). The utility of math difficulties, internalized psychopathology, and visual-spatial deficits to identify children with the nonverbal learning disability syndrome: Evidence for a visual-spatial disability. *Child Neuropsychology, 10*(2), 129–146.

Forrest, B. (2007). Diagnosing and treating right hemisphere disorders. In S. J. Hunter & J. Donders (Eds.), *Pediatric neuropsychological intervention* (pp. 175–192). UK: Cambridge University Press.

Foss, J. (1991). Nonverbal learning disabilities and remedial interventions. *Annuals of Dyslexia, 41*, 128–140.

Francks, C., Paracchini, S., Smith, S. D., Richardson, A. J., Scerri, T. S., Cardon, L. R., et al. (2004). A 77-kilobase region of chromosome 6p22.2 is associated with dyslexia in families from the United Kingdom and from the United States. *American Journal of Human Genetics, 15*, 1046–1058.

Fuchs, L. S., & Fuchs, D. (2006). The role of assessment in the three-tier approach to reading instruction. In D. Haager, J. K. Klingner, & S. Vaughn (Eds.), *Evidence-based reading practices for response to intervention* (pp. 29–42). Baltimore: Paul H Brookes Publishing.

Fuerst, D. R., Fisk, J. L., & Rourke, B. P. (1989). Psychosocial functioning of learning-disabled children: Replicability of statistically derived subtypes. *Journal of Consulting and Clinical Psychology, 57*, 275–280.

Fuerst, D. R., Fisk, J. L., & Rourke, B. P. (1990). Psychosocial functioning of learning disabled children: Relations between WISC verbal IQ-performance IQ discrepancies and personality subtypes. *Journal of Consulting and Clinical Psychology, 58*, 657–660.

Gadow, K. D., DeVincent, C. J., & Schneider, J. (2008). Predictor of psychiatric symptoms in children with autism spectrum disorder. *Journal of Autism and Developmental Disorders, 38*, 1710–1720.

Galaburda, A. M., Sherman, G. F., Rosen, G. D., Aboitiz, F., & Geschwind, N. (1985). Developmental dyslexia: Four consecutive patients with cortical anomalies. *Annals of Neurology, 18*, 222.

Gardner, H. (1999). *Intelligence reframed: Multiple intelligences for the 21st century*. New York: Basic Books.

Geary, D. C. (2000a). Mathematical disorders: An overview for educators. *Perspectives, 26*, 6–9.

Geary, D. C. (2000b). Mathematical disorders: An overview for educators. *Perspectives, 26*(3), 6–9.

Geller, D., Donnelly, C., Lopez, F., Rubin, R., Newcorn, J., Sutton, V., et al. (2007). Atomoxetine treatment for pediatric patients with attention-deficit/hyperactivity disorder with comorbid anxiety disorder. *Journal of the American Academy of Child and Adolescent Psychiatry, 46*(9), 1119–1127.

Gerstmann, J. (1940). Syndrome of finger agnosia, disorientation for right and left, agraphia and acalculia. *Archives of Neurology and Psychiatry, 44*, 389.

Ghaziuddin, M., Butler, E., Tsai, L., & Ghaziuddin, N. (1994). Is clumsiness a marker for Asperger syndrome? *Journal of Intellectual Disability Research, 38*, 519–527.

Ghaziuddin, M., & Mountain-Kinchi, K. (2004). Defining the intellectual profile of Asperger syndrome: Comparison with high-functioning autism. *Journal of Autism and Developmental Disorders, 34*, 279–284.

Gillberg, C. (1991a). *Autism and Asperger syndrome*. Cambridge: Cambridge University Press.

Gillberg, C. (1991b). *Autism and Asperger syndrome*. Cambridge: Cambridge University Press.

Gioia, G. A., Isquith, P. K., Guy, S. C., & Kentworthy, L. (2000). *Behavior rating inventory of executive function*. Lutz, FL: Psychological Assessment Resources.

Glass, K. L., Guli, L. A., & Semrud-Clikeman, M. (2000). Social competence intervention program: A pilot program for the development of social competence. *Journal of Psychotherapy in Independent Practice Social competence and developmental disorders, 1*(4), 21–33.

Goldberg, J., Anderson, G. M., Zwaigenbaum, L., Hall, G. B. C., Nahmias, C., Thompson, A., et al. (2009). Cortical serotonin type-2 receptor density in parents of children with autism spectrum disorders. *Journal of Autism and Developmental Disorders, 39*(1), 97–104.

Gordan, T. (2006). *Parent effectiveness training*. Solana Beach, CA: Gordon Training International.

Goyette, G. H., Conners, C. K., & Ulrich, R. F. (1978). Normative data on the revised Conners Parent and Teacher Rating Scales. *Journal of Abnormal Child Psychology, 6*, 221–236.

Green, D. (1999). *Growing up with NLD*. Albuquerque, NM: Silicon Heights.

Greenberg, L. M. (1989). *Test of variables of attention (TOVA)*. Los Alamitos, CA: Universal Attention Disorders.

Greenberg, L. M., & Kindschi, C. L. (1996). *Test of variables of attention: Clinical guide*. Los Alamitos, CA: Universal Attention Disorders.

Gresham, F. M. (1990). Best practices in social skills training. In A. Thomas & J. Grimes (Eds.), *Best practices in school psychology* (Vol. 2, pp. 695–709). Washington, DC: National Association of School Psychologists.

Gresham, F. M., & Elliott, S. N. (1989). Social skills assessment technology for LD students. *Learning Disability Quarterly, 12*, 141–152.

Gresham, F. M., & Elliott, S. (1990). *Social skills rating system*. Bloomington, MN: Pearson Assessment.

Gresham, F., Goldberg, E., & Costa, L. D. (1981). Hemisphere differences in the acquisition and use of descriptive systems. *Brain and Language, 14*, 144–173.

Griffin, J., & Gresham, D. (2002). *Binocular anomalies: Diagnosis and vision therapy* (4th ed.). Oxford, UK: Butterworth-Heinemann.

Griffiths, A., Parson, L. B., Burns, M. K., Van Der Heyden, A., & Tilly, W. D. (2007a). *Response to intervention: Research for practice*. Alexandria, VA: National Association of State Directors of Special Education Inc.

Griffiths, A., Parson, L. B., Burns, M. K., Van Der Heyden, A., & Tilly, W. D. (2007b). *Response to intervention: Research for practice*. Alexandria, VA: National Association of State Directors of Special Education Inc.

Grodzinsky, G. M. (2003, March 20–23). *Subtypes of nonverbal learning disability: A neuropsychological analysis*. Presented at the 13th Annual Nelson Butters' West Coast Neuropsychology Conference, San Diego, CA.

Gross-Tsur, V., Shalev, R. S., Manor, O., & Amir, N. (1995). Developmental right-hemisphere syndrome: Clinical spectrum of the nonverbal learning disability. *Journal of Learning Disabilities, 28*(2), 80.

Gross-Tsur, V., Manor, O., & Shalev, R. S. (1996). Development dyscalculia: Prevalence and demographic features. *Development Medicine and Child Neurology, 38*, 25–33.

Guli, L. A. (2005). The effects of creative drama-based intervention for children with deficits in social perception. *Dissertation Abstracts International Section A: Humanities and Social Sciences, 65*(10-A).

Guli, L. A., Wilkinson, A., & Semrud-Clikeman, M. (2008). *Enhancing social competence on the autism spectrum: A drama-based intervention for youth*. Champaign, IL: Research Press.

Hain, L. A. (2008). *Exploration of specific learning disability subtypes differentiated across cognitive, achievement, and emotional/behavioral variables*. Unpublished doctoral dissertation, Philadelphia College of Osteopathic Medicine, Philadelphia.

Hain, L. A., Hale, J. B., & Glass-Kendorski, J. (2009). Comorbidity of psychopathology in cognitive and academic SLS subtypes. In S. G. Pfeifer & G. Rattan (Eds.), *Emotional disorders: A neuropsychological, psychopharmacological, and educational perspective* (pp. 199–226). Middletown, MD: School Neuropsychology Press.

Hale, J. B., & Fiorello, C. A. (2004). *School neuropsychology: A practitioner's handbook*. New York: Guilford Press.

Hale, J. B., Naglieri, J. A., Kaufman, A. S., & Kavale, K. A. (2004). Specific learning disability classification in the new individuals with disabilities education act: The danger of good ideas. *The School Psychologist, 29*, 6–13.

Hale, J. B., Naglieri, J. A., Kaufman, A. S., & Kavale, K. A. (2006). Implementation of IDEA: Using RTI and cognitive assessment methods. *Psychology in the Schools, 43*, 753–770.

Hallahan, D. P., & Kauffman, J. M. (1976). *Introduction to learning disabilities: A psychobehavioral approach*. Englewood Cliffs, NJ: Prentice-Hall.

Hammill, D., & Larsen, S. C. (2009). *Test of written language* (4th ed.). Austin, TX: Pro-Ed.

Harnadek, M., & Rourke, B. P. (1994). Principal identifying features of the syndrome of nonverbal learning disabilities in children. *Journal of Learning Disabilities, 27*, 144–154.

Harrison, C., & Sofronoff, K. (2002). ADHD and parental psychological distress: The role of demographics, child behavioural characteristics, and parental cognitions. *Journal of the American Academy of Child and Adolescent Psychiatry, 41*, 703–711.

Harrison, P. L., & Oakland, T. (2003). *Adaptive behavior assessment system* (2nd ed.). San Antonio, TX: Harcourt Assessment.

Hawi, Z., Segurado, R., Conroy, J., Sheehan, K., Lowe, N., Kirley, A., et al. (2005). Preferential transmission of paternal alleles at risk genes in attention-deficit/hyperactivity disorder. *American Journal of Human Genetics, 77*, 958–965.

Higgins, J. J., Pucilowska, J., Lombardi, R. Q., & Rooney, J. P. (2004). Candidate genes for recessive non-syndromic mental retardation on chromosome 3p (MRTA2A). *Clinical Genetics, 65*, 496–500.

Ivry, R. (1993). Cerebellar involvement in the explicit representation of temporal information. In P. Tallal, A. M. Galaburda, R. R. Llinas, & C. von Euler (Eds.), *Temporal information processing in the nervous system* (pp. 214–230). New York: Annals of the New York Academy of Sciences.

Holder, H. B., & Kirkpatrick, S. W. (1991). Interpretation of emotion from facial expressions in children with and without learning disabilities. *Journal of Learning Disabilities, 24*, 170–177.

Hooper, S. R., & Willis, W. G. (1989). *Learning disability subtyping: Neuropsychological foundations, conceptual models, and issues in clinical differentiation.* New York: Springer-Verlag.

Hooper, S. R., Montgomery, J., Swartz, C., Reed, M. S., Sandler, A. D., Levine, M. D., et al. (1994). Measurement of written language expression. In G. R. Lyon (Ed.), *Frames of reference for the assessment of learning disabilities: New views on measurement issues* (pp. 375–417). Baltimore, MD: Paul H Brookes Publishing.

Humphries, T., Krekewich, K., & Snider, L. (1996). Evidence of nonverbal learning disability among learning disabled boys with sensory integrative dysfunction. *Perceptual and Motor Skills, 82*, 979–987. 1996-05353-045.

Humphries, T., Krekewich, K., & Snider, L. (1996). Evidence of nonverbal learning disability among learning disabled boys with sensory integrative dysfunction. *Perceptual and Motor Skills, 82*, 979–987. 1996-05353-045.

Humphries, T., Cardy, J., Worling, D., & Peets, K. (2004). Narrative comprehension and retelling abilities of children with nonverbal learning disabilities. *Brain and Cognition, 56*, 77–88.

ICD-9-CM. (2008). *The International Classification of Diseases, 9th Revision, Clinical Modification (ICD-9-CM)* (6th ed.). Issued for use beginning October 1, 2008 for federal fiscal year 2009 (FY09). The ICD-9-CM is maintained jointly by the National Center for Health Statistics (NCHS) and the Centers for Medicare & Medicaid Services (CMS).

Inhelder, B., & Piaget, J. (1964). *The early growth of logic in the child.* New York: W. W. Norton & Company.

Inspiration Software, Inc. (2008). *Inspiration.* Beaverton, OR: Inspiration Software.

Jastak, J. F., & Jastak, S. R. (1965). *The wide range achievement test.* Wilmington, DE: Guidance Associates.

Jastak, S., & Wilkinson, G. S. (1984). *Wide range achievement test-Revised.* Wilmington, DE: Jastak Associates.

Jimerson, S. R., Burns, M. K., & Van Der Heyden, A. M. (2007). Response to intervention at school: The science and practice of assessment and intervention. In S. R. Jimerson, M. K. Burns, & A. M. Van Der Heyden (Eds.), *Handbook of response to intervention: The science and practice of assessment and intervention* (pp. 3–9). New York: Springer.

Johnson, D. J. (1987a). Nonverbal learning disabilities. *Pediatric Annals, 16*, 133–141.

Johnson, D. J. (1987b). Nonverbal disorders and related learning disabilities. In D. J. Johnson & J. Blalock (Eds.), *Adults with learning disabilities.* New York: Grune & Stratton.

Johnson, D. J., & Myklebust, H. R. (1967). *Learning disabilities: Educational principles and practices.* New York: Grune & Stratton.

Kavale, K. A., & Forness, S. R. (1987). The far side of heterogeneity: A critical analysis of empirical subtyping research in learning disabilities. *Journal of Learning Disabilities, 20*, 374–382.

Kanner, L. (1943). Autistic disturbances of affective contact. *The Nervous Child, 2*, 217–250.

Kauffman, J. M., & Hallahan, D. P. (2005). *The illusion of full inclusion* (2nd ed.). Austin, TX: Pro-Ed.

Keller, C. E., & Sutton, J. P. (1991). Specific mathematics disorders. In J. E. Obrzut & G. Wl Hynd (Eds.), *Neuropsychological foundations of learning disabilities: A handbook of issues, methods and practice*. San Diego, CA: Academic Press.

Keith, T. Z., Fine, J. G., Taub, G. E., Reynolds, M. R., & Krauzler, J. H. (2006). Higher order, multisample, confirmatory factor analysis of the Wechsler Intelligence Scale for Children – Fourth Edition: What does it measure? *School Psychology Review, 35*(1), 108–127.

Killgore, W. D., Glahn, D. C., & Casasanto, D. J. (2005). Development and validation of the Design Organization Test (DOT): A rapid screening instrument for assessing visuospatial ability. *Journal of Clinical and Experimental Neuropsychology, 27*(4), 449–459.

Kistner, J. A., & Gatlin, D. (1989). Correlates of peer rejection among children with learning disabilities. *Learning Disability Quarterly, 12*, 133–140.

Klin, A., & Volkmar, F. (2003). Asperger syndrome: Diagnosis and external validity. *Child and Adolescent Psychiatric Clinics of North America, 12*, 1–13.

Klin, A., Volkmar, F. R., & Sparrow, S. S. (2000). Diagnostic issues in Asperger syndrome. In A. Klin, F. R. Volkmar, & S. S. Sparrow (Eds.), *Asperger syndrome*. New York: Guilford Press.

Klin, A., Sparrow, S. S., Cicchetti, D. V., & Rourke, B. P. (1995). Validity and neuropsychological characterization of Asperger syndrome: Convergence with nonverbal learning disabilities syndrome. *Journal of Child Psychology and Psychology, 36*, 1127–1140.

Klin, A., Sparrow, S. S., Volkmar, F., Cicchetti, D. V., & Rourke, B. P. (1995). Asperger syndrome. In B. P. Rourke (Ed.), *Syndrome of nonverbal learning disabilities: Neurodevelopmental manifestations* (pp. 93–118). New York: Guilford Press.

Klin, A., Volkmar, F. R., Sparrow, S. S., & Cicchetti, B. P. (1996). Validity and neuropsychological characterization of Asperger syndrome: Convergence with nonverbal learning disabilities syndrome. *Annual Progress in Child Psychiatry and Child Development, 36*, 241–259.

Klin, A., Volkmar, F. R., Sparrow, S. S., Cicchetti, B. P., & Rourke, B. P. (2000b). *Asperger syndrome* (1st ed.). New York: Guilford Press.

Klove, H. (1963). Clinical neuropsychology. In F. M. Forster (Ed.), *The medical clinics of North America*. New York: Saunders.

Kohut, H. (1971). The Analysis of the self. New York: International University Press.

Konig, C., & Magill-Evans, J. (2001). Social and language skills in adolescent boys with Asperger syndrome. *Autism, 5*, 23–36.

Koning, C., & Magill-Evans, J. (2001). Validation of the child and adolescent social perception measure. *Occupational Therapy Journal of Research, 21*, 49–67.

Korhonen, T. T. (1991). Neuropsychological stability and prognosis of subgroups of children with learning disabilities. *Journal of Learning Disabilities, 24*, 48–52.

Korkman, M., Kirk, U., & Kemp, S. (2007). *NEPSY-II: A developmental neuropsychological assessment*. San Antonio, TX: Psychological Corporation.

Korkman, M., Kirk, S., & Kirk, U. (2007). *NEPSY II*. San Antonio, TX: Pearson.

Kovacs, M. (2003). *The children's depression inventory*. North Tonawanda, NY: Multi-Health Systems.

Kowalchuk, B., & King, J. D. (1989). Adult suicide vs. coping with non verbal learning disabilities. *Journal of Learning Disabilities, 22*(3), 177–179.

Kreidler, M. (1996). *Evaluation of the pre/post treating protocol of the perceptual enrichment program*. Unpublished manuscript.

Kronbichler, M., Wimmer, H., Staffen, W., Hutzler, F., Mair, A., & Ladurner, G. (2008). Developmental dyslexia: Gray matter abnormalities in the occipitotemporal cortex. *Human Brain Mapping, 29*, 613–625.

Landau, Y., Gross-Tsur, V., Auerbach, J., Van deer Meere, J., & Shalev, R. (1999). Attention-deficit hiperactivity disorder and development righ-hemisphere syndrome: congruence and incongruence of cognitive and behavioral aspects of attention. *Journal of Child Neurology, 14*, 209–303.

Landau, Y. E., Auerbach, J. G., Gross-Tsur, V., & Shalev, R. S. (2003). Speed of performance of children with developmental right hemisphere syndrome and with attention-deficit hyperactivity disorder. *Journal of Child Neurology, 18*(4), 264–268.

Larson, J. P., Hoien, T., Lundberg, I., & Odegaard, H. (1990). MRI evaluation of the size and symmetry of the planum temporale in adolescents with developmental dyslexia. *Brain and Language, 39,* 289–301.

Lavoie, R. (2005). *It's so much work to be your friend: Helping the child with learning disabilities find social success.* New York: Touchstone.

Lavoie, R. (2005). *It's so much work to be your friend: Helping the child with learning disabilities find social success.* New York: Touchstone.

Lerner, J. (2003). *Learning disabilities: Theories, diagnosis, and teaching strategies* (9th ed.). New York: Houghton Mifflin Company.

Levine, M. (2002). *Educational care* (2nd ed.). Cambridge, MA: Educators Publishing Service.

Liddell, G. A., & Rasmussen, C. (2005). Memory profile of children with nonverbal learning disability. *Learning Disabilities Research and Practice, 20,* 137–141.

Little, S. S. (1993). Nonverbal learning disabilities and socioemotional functioning: A review of recent literature. *Journal of Learning Disabilities, 26,* 653–665.

Little, L. (1999). The misunderstood child: The child with a nonverbal learning disorder. *Journal of the Society of Pediatric Nurses, 4*(3), 113–122.

Little, L. (2002). Middle-class mothers' perceptions of peer victimization of children with Asperger's syndrome and nonverbal learning disorders. *Issues in Comprehensive Pediatric Nursing, 25,* 43–57.

Little, L. (2003). Maternal perceptions of the availability, helpfulness and importance of needs for children with Asperger syndrome and nonverbal learning disorders. *Focus on Autism and Other Developmental Disabilities, 18*(4), 257–267.

Lord, C., & Spence, S. J. (2006). Autism spectrum disorders: Phenotype and diagnosis. In S. O. Moldin & J. L. R. Rubenstein (Eds.), *Understanding autism: From basic neuroscience to treatment* (pp. 1–23). Boca Raton, FL: CRC Press.

Madras, K. B., Miller, G. M., & Fischman, A. J. (2005). The dopamintransporter and attention-deficit/ hyperactivity disorder. *Biological Psychiatry, 57,* 1397–1409.

Mary, D., & Jonathan, B. (1999). Normal planum temporale asymmetry in dyslexics with a magnocellular pathway deficit. *NeuroReport: For Rapid Communication of Neuroscience Research, 10*(3), 607–612.

Mamen, M. (2002). *Nonverbal learning disabilities and their clinical subtypes: Assessment, diagnosis and management.* Ottawa, Ontario, Canada: Centrepointe Professional Services.

Mamen, M. (2006). *Nonverbal learning disabilities and their clinical subtypes: A handbook for parents and professionals – New Edition.* Ottawa, Ontario, Canada: Centrepointe Professional Services.

Mamen, M. (2007). *Understanding nonverbal learning disabilities: A common sense guide for parents and professionals.* London: Jessica Kingsley Press.

Mammarella, I. C., Cornoldi, C., Pazzaglia, F., Toso, C., Grimoldi, M., & Vio, C. (2006). Evidence for a double dissociation between spatial-simultaneous and spatial-sequential working memory in visuospatial (nonverbal) learning disabled children. *Brain and Cognition, 62*(1), 58–67.

Manly, T., Robertson, I. H., Andersen, A. H., & Nimmo-Smith, I. (2001). *Test of everyday attention for children.* Lutz, FL: PAR.

March, J. (1997). *Multidimensional anxiety scale for children.* North Tonawanda, NY: Multi-Health Systems.

Marolda, M. R., & Davidson, P. S. (2000). Mathematical learning profiles and differentiated teaching strategies. Perspectives, 26(3), 10–15.

Martin, M. (2007). *Helping Children with nonverbal learning disabilities to Flourish.* London: Jessica Kingsley Publishers.

Marjiviona, J., & Prior, M. (1995). Comparison of Asperger syndrome and high-functioning autistic children on a test of motor impairment. *Journal of Autism and Developmental Disorders, 25,* 23–39.

Mather, N., Roberts, R., Hammill, D. D., & Allen, E. A. (2008). *Test of orthographic competence.* Austin, TX: Pro-Ed.

Matte, R. R., & Bolaski, J. A. (1998). Nonverbal learning disabilities: An overview. *Intervention in School and Clinic, 34*(1), 39–43.

McGrath, M., & Sullivan, M. (2002). Birth weight, neonatal morbidities, and school age outcomes in full-term and preterm infants. *Issues in Comprehensive Pediatric Nursing, 25*(4), 231–254.

McKinney, J. D. (1984). The search for subtypes of specific learning disability. *Journal of Learning Disabilities, 17*, 43–50.

Mellard, D. R., & Johnson, E. (2007). *RTI: A practitioner's guide to implementing response to intervention.* Thousand Oaks, CA: Corwin Press.

Meyers, J. E., & Meyers, K. R. (1995). *Rey complex figure test and recognition trial (RCFT).* Odessa, FL: Psychological Assessment Resources.

Mokros, H. B., Poznanski, E. O., & Merrick, W. A. (1989). Depression and learning disabilities in children: A test of an hypothesis. *Journal of Learning Disabilities, 22*, 230–244.

Molenaar-Klumper, M. (2002). *Non-verbal learning disabilities: Characteristics, diagnosis and treating within an educational setting.* London: Jessica Kingsley, Publishers.

Moore, I. M., Kramer, J. H., Wara, W., Halberg, F., & Ablin, A. R. (1991). Cognitive function in children with leukemia: Effects of radiation dose and time since treatment. *Cancer, 68*, 1913–1917.

Morgan, A. E. (1997). Anatomical variation of the planum temporale: Implications for dyslexia and linguistic ability. *Dissertation Abstracts International: Section B: The Sciences and Engineering, 57*(7-B), 4773.

Mostofsky, S. H., Reiss, A. L., Lockhart, P., & Denckla, M. B. (1998). Evaluation of cerebellar size in attention-deficit hyperactivity disorder. *Journal of Child Neurology, 13*(9), 434–439.

Murphy, D. G., DeCarli, C. D., Daly, E., Haxby, J. V., Allen, G., White, B. J., et al. (1993). X chromosome effects on female brain: A magnetic resonance imaging study of Turner's syndrome. *Lancet, 342*, 1197–1200.

Myklebust, H. R. (1975). Nonverbal learning disabilities: Assessment and intervention. In H. R. Myklebust (Ed.), *Progress in learning disabilities* (Vol. 3, pp. 85–121). New York: Grune & Stratton.

Nangle, D. W., Erdley, C. A., Newman, J. E., Mason, C. A., & Carpenter, E. M. (2003). Popularity, friendship quantity, and friendship quality: Interactive influences on children's loneliness and depression. *Journal of Clinical Child and Adolescent Psychology, 32*, 546–555.

Naogi, S. M., & McCandliss, B. D. (2006). Left lateralized white matter microstructure accounts for individual differences in reading ability and disability. *Neuropsychologia, 44*(11), 2178–2188.

NewDelman, J. M. (1997). *Construct validation of the neuropsychological syndrome of nonverbal learning disability and the validation of the NewDelman assessment of nonverbal learning disabilities: An instrument to screen for the disorder.* A dissertation submitted in partial fulfillment of the requirements for the degree of Doctor of Philosophy in Psychology, California School of Professional Psychology, Fresno Campus.

Nowicki, S., & Duke, M. (1992). *Helping the child who doesn't fit in.* Atlanta, GA: Peachtree Publishers.

Nowicki, S., & Duke, M. (2002). *Will I ever fit in?* New York: Free Press.

Ostad, S. A. (1998). Comorbidity between mathematics and spelling. *Logopedics, Phoniatrics, Vocology, 23*, 145–154.

Ozols, E. J., & Rourke, B. P. (1985). Dimensions of social sensitivity in two types of learning-disabled children. In B. P. Rourke (Ed.), *Neuropsychology of learning disabilities* (pp. 281–301). New York: Guilford Press.

Ozols, E. J., & Rourke, B. P. (1988). Characteristics of young learning-disabled children classified according to patterns of academic achievement: Auditory-perceptual and visual-perceptual abilities. *Journal of Clinical Child Psychology, 17*, 44–52.

Ozols, E. J., & Rourke, B. P. (1991). Classification of young learning-disabled children according to patterns of academic achievement: Validity studies. In B. P. Rourke (Ed.), *Neuropsychological validation of learning disability subtypes* (pp. 97–123). New York: Guilford Press.

Ozonoff, S., & Rogers, S. J. (2003). Autism spectrum disorders: A research review for practitioners. In S. Ozonoff, S. J. Rogers, & R. L. Hendren (Eds.), *Review of psychiatry* (pp. 3–33). Washington: American Psychiatric.

Ozonoff, S., & Rogers, S. J. (2003). From Kanner to the millennium: Scientific advances that have shaped clinical practice. In S. Ozonoff, S. J. Rogers, & R. L. Hendren (Eds.), *Autism spectrum disorders: A research review for practitioners* (pp. 3–33). New York: American Psychiatric Publishing Inc.

Palombo, J. (2006). *Nonverbal learning disabilities: A clinical perspective.* New York: W.W. Norton.

Palombo, J., & Berenberg, A. H. (1999). Working with parents of children with nonverbal learning disabilities: A conceptual and intervention model. In J. A. Incorvaia, B. S. Mark-Goldstein, & D. Tessmer (Eds.), *Understanding, diagnosing, and treating AD/HD in children and adolescents: An integrated approach* (pp. 389–441). Northvale, NJ: Aronson.

Palombo, J. (2001). The therapeutic process with children with learning disorders. *Psychoanalytic Social Work, 8*(3/4), 143–168.

Pavuluri, M. N., Yang, S., Kamineni, K., Passarotti, A. M., Srinivasan, G., Harral, E. M., et al. (2009). Diffusion tensor imaging study of white matter fiber tracts in pediatric bipolar disorder and attention-deficit/hyperactivity disorder. *Biological Psychiatry, 65*, 586–593.

Pearl, R. (1987). Social cognitive factors in learning disabled children's social problems. In S. J. Ceci (Ed.), *Handbook of cognitive, social, and neuropsychological aspects of learning disabilities* (Vol. 2, pp. 273–294). Hillsdale, NJ: Erlbaum.

Peck, M. (1985). Crisis intervention treatment with chronically and acutely suicidal adolescents. In M. Peck, N. L. Farberow, & R. Litman (Eds.), *Youth suicide.* New York: Springer.

Pelham, W. E., Wheeler, T., & Chronis, A. (1998). Empirically supported psychosocial treatments for ADHD. *Journal of Clinical Child Psychology, 27*, 189–204.

Pelletier, P. M., Ahmad, S. A., & Rourke, B. P. (2001). Classification rules for basic phonological processing disabilities and nonverbal learning disorders. *Child Neuropsychology, 7*, 84–98.

Pennington, B. F. (1991a). *Diagnosing learning disorders: A neuropsychological framework.* New York: Guilford Press.

Pennington, B. (2009). *Diagnosing learning disorders* (2nd ed.). New York, Guilford Press.

Pennington, B. F. (2009). *Diagnosing learning disorders* (2nd ed.). New York: Guilford Press.

Pennington, G. F., Bender, B., Puck, M., Salbenblatt, J., & Robinson, A. (1982). Learning disabilities in children with sex chromosome anomalies. *Child Development, 53*, 1182–1192.

Perlmutter, B. F. (1986). Personality variables and peer relations of children and adolescents with learning disabilities. In S. J. Ceci (Ed.), *Handbook of cognitive, social, and neuropsychological aspects of learning disabilities* (Vol. 1, pp. 339–359). Hillsdale, NJ: Erlbaum.

Phelps-Terasaki, D., & Phelps-Gunn, T. (2007). *Test of pragmatic language* (2nd ed.). Greenville, SC: SuperDuper Publications.

Piaget, J. (1972). *The psychology of intelligence.* Totowa, NJ: Littlefield Adams.

Picard, E. M., & Rourke, B. P. (1995). Neuropsychological consequences of prophylactic treatment for acute lymphocytic leukemia. In B. P. Rourke (Ed.), *Syndrome of nonverbal learning disabilities: Neurodevelopmental manifestations* (pp. 282–330). New York: Guilford Press.

Porter, J. E., & Rourke, B. P. (1985). Socioemotional functioning of learning disabled children: A subtypal analysis of personality patterns. In B. P. Rourke (Ed.), *Neuropsychology of learning disabilities: Essentials of subtype analysis.* New York: Guilford Press.

Potter, A. S., Newhouse, P. A., & Bucci, D. J. (2006). Central nicotinic cholinergic systems: A role in the cognitive dysfunction in attention-deficit/hyperactivity disorder? *Behavioural Brain Research, 175*(2), 201–211.

Prasad, H. C., Steiner, J. A., Sutcliffe, J. S., & Blakely, R. D. (2009). Enhanced activity of human serotonin transporter variants associated with autism. *Philosophical Transactions of the Royal Society of London. Series B: Biological Sciences, 364*, 163–173.

Press, G. A., Murakami, J., Courchesne, E., Grafe, M., & Hesselink, J. R. (1990). The cerebellum, 3: Anatomic-MR correlation in the coronal plane. *American Journal of Neuroradiology, 11*, 41–50.

Prior, M., Smart, D., Sanson, A., & Oberlaid, F. (1999). Relationships between learning difficulties and psychological problems in preadolescent children from a longitudinal sample. *Journal of the American Academy of Child and Adolescent Psychiatry, 38*, 429–436.

Quay, H. D., & Peterson, D. R. (1979). *Manual for the behavior problem checklist.* Available from Dr. H. Quay, Department of Psychology, University of Miami, Coral Gables, FL 33124.

Reed, L. E. (2001). *Unaware: Living with non-verbal learning disabilities.* Self published.

Reitan, R. (1969). *Manual for administration of neuropsychological test batteries for adults and children.* Unpublished manuscript, Indianapolis University Medical Center.

Reynolds, C. R., & Kamphaus, R. W. (2004). *Behavior assessment scale for children (BASC-2)* (2nd ed.). Bloomington, MN: AGS Publishing.

Roberts, G. (2001). *Roberts apperception test for children and adolescents* (2nd ed.). Los Angeles, CA: Western Psychological Services.

Robichon, F., Levrier, O., Farnarier, P., & Habib, M. (2000). Developmental dyslexia: Atypical cortical asymmetries and functional significance. *European Journal of Neurology, 7*(1), 35–46.

Roid, G. H. (2003). *Stanford-Binet intelligence scale* (5th ed.). Itasca, IL: Riverside.

Roman, M. A. (1998). The syndrome of nonverbal learning disabilities: Clinical description and applied aspects. *Current Issues in Education (CIE).* 1:1.

Ross, E. D. (2000). Affective prosody and the aprosodias. In M. M. Mesulam (Ed.), *Principles of behavioral and cognitive neurology* (2nd ed.). UK: Oxford University Press.

Rourke, B. P. (Ed.). (1985). *Neuropsychology of learning disabilities: Essentials of subtype analysis.* New York: Guilford Publications.

Rourke, B. P. (1988). The syndrome of nonverbal learning disabilities: Developmental manifestations in neurological disease and dysfunction. *The Clinical Neuropsychologist, 4*, 293–330.

Rourke, B. P. (1989). *Nonverbal learning disabilities: The syndrome and the model.* New York: Guilford Press.

Rourke, B. P. (1995). The NLD syndrome and the white matter model. In B. P. Rourke (Ed.), *Syndrome of nonverbal learning disabilities: Neurodevelopmental manifestations.* New York: Guilford Press.

Rourke, B. P. (2000). Nonverbal learning disabilities. In A. Klin, F. R. Volkmar, & S. S. Sparrow (Eds.), *Asperger syndrome.* New York: Guildford Press.

Rourke, B. P., Ahmad, S. A., Collins, D. W., Hayman-Abello, S. E., & Warriner, E. M. (2002). Child clinical/pediatric neuropsychology: Some recent advances. *Annual Review of Psychology, 53*, 309–339.

Rourke, B. P., & Strang, J. D. (1978). Neuropsychological significance of variations in patterns of academic performance: Motor, psychomotor, and tactile-perceptual abilities. *Journal of Pediatric Psychology, 3*, 62–66.

Rourke, B. P., & Tsatsanis, K. D. (1996). Syndrome of nonverbal learning disabilities: Psycholinguistic assets and deficits. *Topics in Language Disorders, 16*(2), 30–44.

Rourke, B. P., Young, G. C., & Leenaars, A. A. (1989). A childhood learning disability that predisposes those afflicted to adolescent and adult depression and suicide risk. *Journal of Learning Disabilities, 22*(3), 169–173.

Sacco, R., Militerni, R., Frolli, A., Bravaccio, C., Gritti, A., Elia, M., et al. (2007). Clinical, morphological, and biochemical correlates of head circumference in autism. *Biological Psychiatry, 62*(9), 1038–1047.

Schiff, R., Bauminger, N., & Toledo, I. (2009). Analogical problem solving in children with verbal and nonverbal learning disabilities. *Journal of Learning Disabilities, 42*, 3–13.

Schloerb, A. P. (2005). The impact of nonverbal learning disabilities on early development. *Praxis, 5*, 55–60.

Schopler, E. (1996). Are autism and Asperger syndrome different labels or different disabilities? *Journal of Autism and Developmental Disorders, 26*, 109–110.

Schopler, E., Mesibov, G. B., & Kunce, L. J. (1998). *Asperger syndrome or high-functioning autism.* New York: Plenum Publishing Corporation.

Schultz, R. T., Romanski, L. M., & Tsatsanis, K. D. (2000). Neurofunctional models of autistic disorder and Asperger syndrome: Clues from neuroimaging. In A. Klin, F. R. Volkmar, & S. S. Sparrow (Eds.), *Asperger syndrome*. New York: Guilford Press.

Semrud-Clikeman, M. (2001). *Traumatic brain injury in children and adolescents*. New York: Guilford Press.

Semrud-Clikeman, M. (2003). Executive functions and social communication disorders. *Perspectives, 29*, 20–22.

Semrud-Clikeman, M. (2007). *Social competence in children*. New York: Springer.

Semrud-Clikeman, M. (2009). Personal Communication.

Semrud-Clikeman, M., & Fine, J. (2011). Presence of cysts on magnetic resonance images (MRIs) in children with Asperger disorder and nonverbal learning disabilities. *Journal of Child Neurology, 11*, 1–5.

Semrud-Clikeman, M., Fine, J. G., & Bledsoe, J. (2008a). *Meta-analysis of empirical literature on NVLD*. Paper presented at the International Neuropsychological Society.

Semrud-Clikeman, M., Fine, J. G., & Bledsoe, J. (2008b). *Meta-analysis of empirical research in assessment and diagnosis in NVLD*. Paper presented at the International Neuropsychological Association.

Semrud-Clikeman, M., & Glass, K. L. (2008). Comprehension of humor in children with nonverbal learning disabilities, Verbal learning disabilities and without learning disabilities. *Annals of Dyslexia, 58*, 163–180.

Semrud-Clikeman, M., & Hynd, G. W. (1990). Right hemisphere dysfunction in nonverbal learning disabilities: Social, academic, and adaptive functioning in adults and children. *Psychological Bulletin, 107*(2), 196–209.

Semrud-Clikeman, M., & Hynd, G. W. (1990). Right hemispheric dysfunction in nonverbal learning disabilities: Social, academic, and adaptive functioning in adults and children. *Psychological Bulletin, 197*, 196–209.

Semrud-Clikeman, M., & Schaefer, V. (2000). Social competence in developmental disorders. *Journal of Psychotherapy in Independent Practice, 4*, 3–20.

Semrud-Clikeman, M., & Schafer, V. (2000). Social and emotional competence in children with ADHD and/or learning disabilities. *Journal of Psychotherapy in Independent Practice, 1*(4), 3–19.

Semrud-Clikeman, M., Walkowiak, J., Wilkinson, A., & Christopher, G. (2010). Neuropsychological differences among children with Asperger syndrome, nonverbal learning disabilities, attention deficit disorder, and controls. *Developmental Neuropsychology, 35*(5), 582–600.

Semrud-Clikeman, M., Walkowiak, J., Wilkinson, A., & Minne, E. P. (2010). Behavior and social perception in children with Asperger's disorder, nonverbal learning disability, or ADHD. *Journal of Abnormal Child Psychology, 38*, 509–519.

Semrud-Clikeman, M., & Hynd, G. W. (1990). Right hemispheric dysfunction in nonverbal learning disabilities: Social, academic, and adaptive functioning in adults and children. *Psychological Bulletin, 197*, 196–209.

Semrud-Clikeman, M., & Glass, K. (2008). Comprehension of humor in children with nonverbal learning disabilities, verbal learning disabilities and without learning disabilities. *Annals of Dyslexia, 58*, 163–180.

Shalev, R. S. (2004). *Developmental dyscalculia:Review. Journal of Child Neurology, 19*, 765–771.

Sheslow, D., & Adams, W. (2003). *Wide range assessment for memory and learning* (2nd ed.). Lutz, FL: Psychological Assessment Resources.

Silver, C. H., Ring, J., Pennett, D., & Black, J. L. (2007). Verbal and visual short-term memory in children with arithmetic disabilities. *Developmental Neuropsychology, 32*, 847–860.

Simon, T. J. (2007). Cognitive characteristics of children with genetic syndromes. *Child and Adolescent Psychiatric Clinics of North America, 16*, 599–616.

Simon, T. J. (2008). A new account of the neurocognitive foundations of impairments in space, time and number processing in children with chromosome 22q11.2 deletion syndrome. *Developmental Disabilities Research Reviews, 14*, 48–58.

Soriano, F. I. (1995). *Conducting needs assessments: A multidisciplinary approach.* Thousand Oaks, CA: Sage.

Sparrow, S. S., Cicchetti, D. V., & Balla, P. A. (2004). *Vineland adaptive behavior scales* (2nd ed.). Bloomington, MN: Pearson Assessment.

Spreen, O. (1988). *Learning disabled children growing up.* New York: Oxford University Press.

Spreen, O., & Strauss, E. (1998). *A compendium of neuropsychological tests: Administration, norms, and commentary* (2nd ed.). New York: Oxford University Press.

Stahl, S. A. (1999). *Vocabulary development.* Newton Upper Falls, MA: Brookline Books.

Stanfield, A. C., McIntosh, A. M., Spencer, M. D., Philip, R., Gaur, S., & Lawrie, S. M. (2008). Towards a neuroanatomy of autism: A systematic review and meta-analysis of structural magnetic resonance imaging studies. *European Psychiatry, 23*(4), 289–299.

Stefanatos, G. A., & Wasserstein, J. (2001). Attention deficit hyperactivity disorder as a right hemisphere syndrome: Selective review and detailed neuropsychological case studies. *Annals of the New York Academy of Sciences, 931*, 172–195.

Stern, D. (2000). *The interpersonal world of the infant: A view from psychoanalysis and developmental psychology.* New York: Basic Books.

Steinlin, M. (2007). The cerebellum in cognitive processes: Supporting studies in children. *Cerebellum, 6*(3), 237–241.

Szatmari, P. (1998). Differential diagnosis of Asperger disorder. In E. Schopler, G. B. Mesibov, & L. J. Kunce (Eds.), *Asperger syndrome or high-functioning autism?* (pp. 61–76). New York: Plenum.

Szatmari, P., Saigal, S., Rosenbaum, P., Campbell, D., & Susanne, K. (1990). Psychiatric disorders at five years among children with birthweights <1000g: A regional perspective. *Developmental Medicine and Child Neurology, 32*(11), 954–962.

Tanguay, P. B. (2001). *Nonverbal learning disabilities at home.* London: Jessica Kingsley, Publishers.

Tanguay, P. B. (2002). *Nonverbal learning disabilities at school.* London: Jessica Kingsley, Publishers.

Tannock, R., Martinussen, R., & Frijters, J. (2000). Naming speed performance and stimulant effects indicate effortful, semantic processing deficits in attention-deficit/hyperactivity disorder. *Journal of Abnormal Child Psychology, 28*(3), 237–252.

Tastsanis, K. D., & Rourke, B. P. (1995). Conclusions and future directions. In B. P. Rourke (Ed.), *Syndrome of nonverbal learning disabilities* (pp. 476–496). New York: Guilford Press.

Teeter, A. T., & Semrud-Clikeman, M. (1997). *Child neuropsychology: Assessment and interventions for neurodevelopmental disorders.* Needham Heights, MA: Allyn & Bacon.

Telzrow, C. F., & Bonar, A. M. (2002). Responding to students with nonverbal learning disabilities. *Teaching Exceptional Children, 34*, 8–13.

Ternes, J., Woody, R., & Livingston, R. (1987). Case report: A child with right hemisphere deficit syndrome responsive to carbamazepine treatment. *Journal of Child and Adolescent Psychiatry, 26*(4), 586–588.

Thompson, S. (1997). *The source for nonverbal learning disorders.* East Moline, IL: Linguisystems.

Tiffin, J. (1968). *Purdue pegboard: Examiner manual.* Chicago: Science Research Associates.

Torgesen, J., Wagner, R., & Rashotte, C. (1999). *Test of word reading efficiency.* Minneapolis, MN: Pearson.

Trites, R. (1995). *Grooved pegboard test.* Lafayette, IN: Lafayette Instrument.

Tsatsanis, K. D., & Rourke, B. P. (2003). Syndrome of nonverbal learning disabilities: Effects on learning. In A. H. Fine & R. Kotkin (Eds.), *Therapists guide to learning and attention disorders* (pp. 109–145). New York: Academic Press.

Tsatsanis, K. D., Fuerst, D. R., & Rourke, B. P. (1997). Psychosocial dimensions of learning disabilities: External validation and relationships with age and academic functioning. *Journal of Learning Disabilities, 30*, 490–502.

Vaivre-Douret, L., Lalanne, C., Mouchel, B., Ingster-Moati, I., Boddaert, N., et al. (in press). Subtypes of developmental dyspraxia and developmental coordination disorder: Research on their etiology. *Journal of Clinical and Experimental Neuropsychology.*

Voeller, K. K. (1995). Clinical neurological aspects of the right hemisphere deficit syndrome. *Journal of Child Neurology, 10,* 16–22.

Voeller, K. K. S. (1986). Right-hemisphere deficit in children. *The American Journal of Psychiatry, 143,* 1004–1009.

Volden, J. (2004). Nonverbal learning disability: A tutorial for speech-language pathologists. *American Journal of Speech-Language Pathology, 13,* 128–141.

Volkmar, F. R., & Klin, A. (1998). Asperger syndrome and nonverbal learning disabilities. In E. Schopler, G. B. Mesibov, & L. J. Kunce (Eds.), *Asperger syndrome or high-functioning autism? Current issues in autism* (pp. 107–121). New York: Plenum.

Volkmar, F. R., & Klin, A. (2000). Diagnostic issues in Asperger syndrome. In A. Klin, F. R. Volkmar, & S. S. Sparrow (Eds.), *Asperger syndrome.* New York: Guilford Press.

Wagner, R. K., Torgesen, J. K., & Roshotte, C. A. (1999). *Comprehensive test of phonological processing.* Austin, TX: Pro-Ed.

Walther, F. J., den Ouden, A. L., & Verloove-Vanhorick, S. P. (2000). Looking back in time: Outcome of a national cohort of very preterm infants born in The Netherlands in 1983. *Early Human Development, 59*(3), 175–191.

Wechsler, D. (1991). *Wechsler intelligence scale for children* (3rd ed.). San Antonio: The Psychological Corporation.

Wechsler, D. (1997). *Wechsler memory scales, examiner's manual* (3rd ed.). San Antonio, TX: The Psychological Corporation.

Wechsler, D. (2003). *Wechsler intelligence scale for children (WISC-IV)* (4th ed.). San Antonio, TX: The Psychological Corporation.

Wechsler, A. F. (2008). *Wechsler adult intelligence scale* (4th ed.). San Antonio, TX: Arcourt Assessment.

Weiderholt, J. L., & Bryant, B. R. (2001). *Gray oral reading test* (4th ed.). Austin, TX: Pro-Ed.

Weintraub, S., & Mesulam, M. M. (1983). *Archives of Neurology, 40,* 463–468.

Weintraub, S., & Mesulam, M. M. (1983). Developmental learning disabilities of the right hemisphere. *Archives of Neurology, 40,* 463–468.

Weintraub, S., & Mesulam, M. M. (1983). Developmental learning disabilities of the right hemisphere. Emotional, interpersonal, and cognitive components. *Archives of Neurology, 11,* 463–468.

Wellington, T. M., Semrud-Clikeman, M., Gregory, A. L., Murphy, J. M., & Lancaster, J. L. (2006). Magnetic resonance imaging volumetric analysis of the putamen in children with ADHD: Combined type versus control. *Journal of Attention Disorders, 10*(2), 171–180.

White, J. L., Moffitt, T. E., & Silva, P. A. (1992). Neuropsychological and socio-emotional correlates of specific-arithmetic disability. *Archives of Clinical Neuropsychology, 7,* 1–16.

White, R. F., & Rose, F. E. (1997). The Boston process approach: A brief history and current practice. In G. Goldstein & T. M. Incagnoli (Eds.), *Contemporary approaches to neuropsychological assessment* (pp. 171–212). New York: Plenum Press.

Whitney, R. V. (2000). *The nonverbal learning disorder guide for teachers, parents, employers, and therapists.* Campbell, CA: Lighthouse Project.

Whitney, R. V. (2002). *Bridging the gap: Raising a child with nonverbal learning disorder.* New York: Penguin Putnam.

Wiig, E. H., & Secord, W. (1989). *Test of language competence – Expanded edition.* San Antonio, TX: The Psychological Corporation.

Wilens, T. E. (2009). *Straight talk about psychiatric medications for kids* (3rd ed.). New York: Guilford Press.

Willcutt, E. G., Pennington, B. F., & DeFries, J. C. (2000). Etiology of inattention and hyperactivity/impulsivity in a community sample of twins with learning difficulties. *Journal of Abnormal Child Psychology, 28*(2), 149–159.

Wilkinson, A., & Semrud-Clikeman, M. (2008). *Motor speed in children and adolescents with nonverbal learning disabilities.* Paper presented at the International Neuropsychological Society.

Wirt, R. D., Lachar, D., Klinedinst, J. K., & Seat, P. D. (1977). *Multidimensional dexription of chlid personality: A manual for the personality inventory for children.* Los Angeles: Western Psychological Services.

Wolff, S. (1995). *Loners: The life path of unusual children.* London: Routledge.

Woodin, M., Wang, P. P., Aleman, D., McDonald-McGinn, D., Zackai, E., & Moss, E. (2001). Neuropsychological profile of children and adolescents with the 22q11.2 microdeletion. *Genetics in Medicine, 3,* 34–39.

Woodbury, M. (1993). Recurrent abdominal pain in child patients seen at a pediatric gastroenterology clinic: Observations of 50 children and their families. *Psychosomatics, 34*(6), 486–493.

Woodcock, R. W., McGrew, K. S., & Mather, N. (2001). *Woodcock-Johnson III tests of achievement.* Itasca, IL: Riverside.

Worling, D. E., Humphries, T., & Tannock, R. (1999). Spatial and emotional aspects of language inferencing in nonverbal learning disabilities. *Brain and Language, 70,* 220–239.

Yell, M. L. (2006). *The law and special education* (2nd ed.). Upper Saddle River, NJ: Pearson Education Inc.

About the Authors

John M. Davis, Ph.D., is currently an Associate Professor at California State University, East Bay, and Chair of the Educational Psychology Department, where he teaches and supervises. He received his Ph.D. from the U.C. Berkeley School Psychology program and did clinical postdoctoral studies to become a licensed psychologist. He has a special interest in learning and developmental disorders having been the director of a school and clinic for students with learning disabilities for 13 years, which provided diagnostic and intervention services. His current clinical work is primarily with children and adults with learning disorders. His writing and research interests include articles and book chapters in the areas of mental health consultation, suicide/crisis intervention, and learning disorders.

Jessica Broitman, Ph.D., is the President emeritus of the San Francisco Psycho-therapy Research Group and Executive Director of its Clinic and Training Center. She frequently lectures on Weiss's Control Mastery Theory worldwide. A psychoanalyst in private practice since 1980, she has worked with families who have learning-disabled children for more than 10 years. She is currently involved in several research projects concerning the treatment and understanding of NVLD and has a special interest in helping professionals and families understand and treat this disorder.

Index

CPSIA information can be obtained at www.ICGtesting.com

229921LV00003B/15/P

9 781441 982124